Economic Analysis
and
Industrial Structure

Economics Series
Under the Editorship of
Clark W. Reynolds
Stanford University

READINGS IN MICROECONOMICS
edited by
William Breit and Harold M. Hochman,
University of Virginia

ECONOMIC ANALYSIS AND INDUSTRIAL STRUCTURE
Douglas Needham,
*The London School of Economics and Political Science,
University of London*

Economic Analysis and Industrial Structure

DOUGLAS NEEDHAM
The London School of Economics
and Political Science,
University of London

HOLT, RINEHART AND WINSTON, INC.
New York   Chicago   San Francisco   Atlanta
Dallas   Montreal   Toronto   London   Sydney

Copyright © 1969 by Holt, Rinehart and Winston, Inc.
Library of Congress Catalog Card Number: 69-17656
SBN: 03–076550–1
Printed in the United States of America
1 2 3 4 5 6 7 8 9

To Linda

EDITOR'S FOREWORD

With the appearance of this textbook a new series is inaugurated which, it is hoped, will answer the challenge of those who find the present state of undergraduate education in economics less than satisfactory. The public has demanded greater relevance of courses and readings to the pressing social issues of our time, yet without loss of theoretical content. It has requested greater openness of methodology to the insights of other branches of the social sciences, yet without the sacrifice of rigor. Indeed, what appears to be required is an expansion of the dimensions of the theoretical apparatus which economics has pioneered so as to embrace a broader set of social variables in which economic "general equilibrium" theory is explicitly relegated to a position it has always held by assumption, that of partial equilibrium social theory. At the present time this mandate makes sense only as a statement of intent, since much of economic theory remains fragmentary, compartmentalized, and scarcely subject to reconciliation within the confines of its own assumptions, much less within a broader framework of social equilibrium theory yet to be devised.

The volumes in this series are therefore designed to present conventional economic theory in as eclectic as possible a manner such that its usefulness in new areas of analysis will be maximized, while at the same time preserving methodological precision. *Economic Analysis and Industrial Structure* is a prime example of this new look in economics. It analyzes the behavioral determinants of firm and industrial structure and their implications for pricing and production policies from a broad philosophical and methodological perspective. The firm is not regarded as a predetermined historical institution to be studied as a *fait accompli*. Instead it is seen to evolve subject to interacting economic and social forces which bring about its rise or fall, merger or fragmentation, even as the business unit itself influences the economy and society. It is this broader analytical framework to which the readers' attention is directed —those wishing to discover why monopolies occur, why some firms compete with prices and others with advertising or innovation, why mergers take place, why bankruptcy is prevalent in some industries, and what determines the major trends in industrial structure will find an able introduction to these questions in the following pages.

Each chapter defines a basic problem in industrial organization analysis and then develops the tools for its analysis in terms of alternative maximizing criteria and reaction paths of the firm and the industry. Alternative methods of measuring the variables are examined for the benefit of those interested in further hypothesis testing. A bibliography of readings is appended to each section, leading readers into more advanced work on the subject, and weak points in the literature are frankly pointed out. Every taste is thereby gratified from the most theoretical to the most practical, without the use of more than elementary mathematics and with verbal description of each major point.

Highlights of the analysis include a dynamic treatment of the firm as a decision-making unit subject to multiple objectives in Chapter One; the employment of substitutability criteria for the definition of industries and a comparison of alternative standard industrial classificatory schemes in Chapter Two; and alternative methods of estimating long-run cost curves and their results together with an agnostic view of u-shaped long-run average cost curves in Chapter Three. A lucid treatment of discriminatory pricing in theory and practice appears in Chapter Four; the following chapter analyzes the economic implications of product differentiation along with the effect of product changes on scale economies and seller concentration. This chapter also deals with the cumulative relationship between firm size and research and development, and product innovation, as well as the trade-off between advertising and innovations as alternative product differentiation strategies. Chapter Six considers the relationship between seller concentration and market behavior. Chapter Seven on barriers to entry goes beyond the assumption of no retaliation to deal with the implications of alternative seller reaction paths for industry pricing and output. The analysis opens up new dimensions of entrepreneurial psychology which have hitherto been somewhat neglected in the textbook literature.

Vertical integration is treated in Chapter Eight in terms of the effect of alternative goals of profit and sales maximization on the extent of integration and its influence on pricing and output. Chapter Nine analyzes diversification as a hedge against uncertainty in terms of the scale and concentration of the receiving industry and as an alternative strategy to vertical integration. Finally in Chapter Ten the principle of Pareto optimality is used to determine the welfare effect of alternative industrial structures and resulting policy implications. This section is of particular interest to businessmen, government officials, students, and others concerned with the influence of industrial structure and policy on the public interest. The merits of pure competition versus monopoly are dealt with subject to qualifications of the theory of the "second best," along with the welfare implications of price agreements, mergers, advertising, research and development expenditures.

The reader will discover that one need not abandon analytical rigor or quantitative methods of hypothesis testing in order to cover a much broader area of industrial organization theory than has traditionally been available in textbook literature. While little more than an introduction is provided to some of the basic issues in the text, Professor Needham opens the door to a wealth of new material which commands the attention of informed laymen as well as those planning to continue in the social sciences. For these reasons this volume has been chosen as a foundation for what is hoped will be a revolutionizing series of textbooks in political economy.

Clark W. Reynolds

PALO ALTO, CALIFORNIA
MARCH 1969

PREFACE

This book is primarily intended to serve as a basic text for a course in industrial organization; it can also be used as an advanced supplementary text in a traditional price theory course.

The focus of the book is upon the role of business firms in influencing, and being influenced by, industrial structure. In most existing industrial organization texts, emphasis is upon structure as a determinant of the pricing behavior of firms. This book attempts to present a more balanced analysis by emphasizing that structural features, including, for example, product differentiation and entry barriers, are to a large extent under the firms' control. Some aspects of the pricing behavior of firms are more fully developed than in existing industrial organization texts and many price theory texts. In addition, the interdependence of pricing and other aspects of a firm's behavior, and the significance of this interdependence both for the firms' behavior and for public policy affecting industrial structure, receives greater emphasis.

The book concentrates upon providing the reader with an analytical peg upon which to hang his empirical knowledge. References to empirical studies are included, but empirical data are omitted from the text entirely. Similarly, those sections of the book dealing with public policy are not concerned with the detailed provisions of the law affecting industrial structure, nor with the way in which the law has been applied in particular cases. It concentrates, instead, upon equipping the reader with a clear understanding of the relevance and limitations of economic analysis in providing a rationale for laws governing pricing, the exchange of information, mergers, and other aspects of firms' behavior.

The book is intended not only for students specializing in economics, but also for lawyers specializing in the field of antitrust and for business school students interested in the determinants of industrial structure and the economic rationale of public policies affecting industrial structure.

Although familiarity with elementary price theory and concepts such as demand, marginal cost, marginal revenue, and elasticity would be helpful to the reader, it is not essential. All such terms used in the text are defined. The book contains no mathematical exposition; the use of mathematics would be inappropriate, given the wide audience the book is intended to serve. Diagrams supplement the verbal exposition where this is likely to aid the reader's understanding.

The book may be used either as an advanced undergraduate text or as a graduate text. If used as a graduate text, it should be extensively supplemented by empirical and analytical articles dealing with particular topics in more detail. Selected readings at the end of each chapter are intended to provide the reader with more detailed treatment of particular topics dealt with in the text.

I wish to thank Basil S. Yamey, Richard M. Cyert, John Williamson, J. R. Gould, and K. G. C. Tan for reading an earlier draft of the book and for making numerous helpful suggestions. Since opinions about the appropriate subject matter of industrial organization are notoriously diverse, I shall not apologize for omissions, and confine the usual apology for any defects that remain to errors.

Douglas Needham

LONDON
FEBRUARY 1969

CONTENTS

CHAPTER ONE

FIRMS, OBJECTIVES, AND INDUSTRIAL STRUCTURE

Meaning of Industrial Structure

The term "structure of industry," as used in this book, refers to a selected number of characteristics of the output of a firm or a group of firms. These characteristics include, for example, cost conditions, concentration, vertical integration, diversification, and entry barriers. Cost conditions describe the relation between the minimum cost of producing and distributing a particular good or service and alternative levels of total output of that product or service. Concentration refers to the number and size distribution of firms producing a particular category of output. Vertical integration refers to the extent to which successive stages in the producing of a particular product or the performing of a service are performed by a single firm. Diversification refers to the extent to which a firm produces different kinds of output not vertically related to one another. Entry barriers are obstacles to a new firm wishing to engage in the production of a particular category of output. A more detailed consideration of the nature and significance of these and other features of industrial structure is postponed until later chapters; first it is appropriate to examine more closely the concept of the firm and the objectives pursued by business enterprises.

Because there are many concepts of the firm, a precise definition is not possible. From an accounting point of view, for example, a firm is a collection of assets and liabilities. From the legal point of view, a firm is either a sole proprietorship, a partnership, or a company with limited liability. Although a firm has many characteristics in addition to those directly relevant to a study of industrial structure, all its characteristics have one thing in common. They are the result of decisions made by people controlling the operations of the firm. All its characteristics are related through the decision-making process. The choice of what to produce, for example, influences the type of assets and liabilities a firm will acquire. The choice of legal form may influence the total amount of investment funds available to the firm and hence the level of its total productive activities. The firm in the sense of a decision-making unit is of primary interest to economists, because they are interested in the determinants of various characteristics of business enterprises and in the relationship between such characteristics, and these are the result of a decision-making process.

Nature of the Firm's Objectives

The structure of industry existing at any point in time may be viewed simply as the result of efforts by thousands of individual decision makers to achieve certain objectives. Productive activity is the process of transforming inputs into outputs. The firm, or rather its decision makers, will select from the alternatives available that combination of inputs and outputs which best achieves the firm's objectives. A list of the many alternative possible objectives pursued by a firm's decision makers would occupy many pages. In the remainder of this section, several of the objectives considered to be of major importance in influencing business behavior, and hence industrial structure, are described.

The first objective to be considered, that of maximizing profits, has for long occupied pride of place in economics textbooks concerned with the behavior of the firm. The word "profits" has many different meanings in everyday usage. In economic analysis, profits are the difference between receipts from the sale of the firm's output(s) and the costs of the inputs required to produce and distribute those outputs. A major distinction is made between profits as a concept in economic analysis and "accounting profits" as measured by traditionally accepted methods of business bookkeeping. In the case of economic profit, the costs of inputs used by a firm are measured by their "opportunity cost," which is defined as the best return an input could earn outside the business, whereas accounting profit measures input costs by the actual money expenditure on inputs. Thus, for example, accounting profit includes the wages an owner-manager could earn by selling his services elsewhere, and also the interest owners of a business could earn elsewhere on the funds they have invested in the business; economic profit, on the other hand, excludes these two items. "Profit maximization" may be interpreted as a desire to maximize the present value of the profits expected from the firm's productive activities over a specific period.

For the benefit of readers unfamiliar with the meaning of present value and the related concept of discounting, a brief digression is appropriate.[1] Discounting, a fundamental concept in the decision-making process, is a process of transforming anticipated future receipts or outlays into equivalent "present values." In order to choose between alternative policies differing from each other in respect to the time path of receipts and outlays associated with each policy, a decision maker must be able to compare receipts and payments occurring at different points in time.

The discounted present value, P, of an amount of receipts or outlays, V, which is expected to accrue after n periods, is defined as

$$P = \frac{V}{(1 + r)^n}$$

where r, called the "discount rate," reflects the decision-maker's own relative evaluation of current versus future receipts or payments. The discount rate is related to the rate of return on the firm's best alternative investment opportunity. It may be related to the rate of interest at which the decision maker can borrow additional funds, or at which he can lend money; alternatively, the discount rate may be related to neither of these rates but instead may reflect the anticipated rate of return on the internal use of the firm's own financial resources. If, for example, the firm can borrow or lend any amount at a given rate of interest, i, the discount rate will equal this rate, because the best alternative to the use of money in the firm is in these circumstances the rate of interest that would be saved by not borrowing the money or that would be earned by lending the money. If the firm can lend at rate i, the "present value" of an amount of receipts, V, accruing one period from now is $V/(1 + i)$, because this expression indicates the amount of money which, if lent now at a rate i would grow to equal V after one period. If the cost of borrowing money increases with the amount borrowed, the discount rate is related to the *marginal* cost of borrowing, rather than to the average cost in terms of the interest rate paid on additional funds. If the firm cannot borrow or lend additional funds, the discount rate is related to the marginal return of money in the most profitable internal use available. In these circumstances the appropriate discount rate for determining discounted present values itself depends upon the best internal use that can be made of the funds. In other words, the discount rate depends upon the optimal calculation and vice versa.

---

[1] Those already familiar with discounting may skip this paragraph and the following one. The reader interested in a more detailed treatment of discounting may consult the articles by Baumol (4), Mishan (9), and Solomon (12) listed at the end of this chapter.

Even in those cases in which the objectives of a firm's decision makers is not maximization of profits, the desire to make some profits will nonetheless usually enter into the decision-maker's objectives for one or both of the following reasons. First, making some profits may be necessary to enable the decision maker to achieve some other objective. Second, all objectives are subject to the constraint of some minimum benefits to the owners of the firm. This constraint may take the form of paid-out profits to owners, considered necessary perhaps by those currently controlling the firm's operations in order to permit them to remain in control. If dividends fall below a certain level, control may be lost because existing shareholders either replace the managers or alternatively sell out to new owners who in turn might install a new management in the hope that the latter would distribute higher dividends. The profit constraint need not, however, necessarily involve paid-out profits; if profits are retained in the business, thereby increasing the firm's net assets and profit-earning potential, owners may experience benefits in the form of capital appreciation of ownership claims.

Rather than attempt to maximize profits, a firm's decision makers may seek to maximize sales revenue, subject to the constraint that profits equal or exceed a certain amount. A number of reasons have been advanced to explain why a firm's decision makers should be more concerned with sales revenues than with profits. It has been argued, for example, that in firms in which ownership is divorced from control, the remuneration of professional managers controlling the firm's operations is linked more closely with sales than with profits. The evidence obtained in a number of empirical studies[2] lends some support to this hypothesis. The higher correlation of executive remuneration with sales than with profits will, it is argued, motivate managers to produce and market levels of output larger than those which maximize profits.

If decision makers pursue maximum sales revenue subject to a profit constraint, the crucial question is what determines the minimum acceptable amount of profit? In a single-period analysis of the sales-revenue-maximizing objective, the profit constraint must be arbitrarily imposed; thus, in the early literature dealing with this objective, it was assumed that the profit constraint was imposed by the capital market and the need to pay owners a return comparable with that paid by other firms in the economy. With a multiperiod analysis in which the decision-maker's objectives are interpreted as the desire to maximize the present value of sales revenue over a specified period of time, however, the profit constraint may be generated automatically by the desire to finance growth of sales revenue. For reasons to be explained later, a sales

---

[2] See, for example, reference (8), J. W. McGuire *et al.*

revenue maximizer will forgo current profits in order to expand current sales revenues beyond the profit-maximizing level. However, current profits enable sales revenue to be expanded in later periods. The choice, in brief, is between larger current sales revenue and lower profits, growing at a slower rate through time; and smaller current sales revenue and higher profits, growing at a faster rate through time. The sales revenue maximizer will choose that combination of current sales and growth rate which maximizes the present value of sales revenue. This combination may involve a positive growth rate of sales revenue, which implies a positive level of profits since profits are necessary to obtain finance for growth.

Apart from the profit constraint that may be generated automatically by a desire to finance expanded output and sales revenue in the future, there may be an additional constraint in the form of a minimum paid-out profit constraint considered necessary by the firm's decision-making unit in order to prevent take-over of the firm and loss of control by the present decision-making unit. With such a paid-out profit constraint, the locus of maximum attainable current-sales–growth-rate combinations is reduced, and the optimal decision which satisfies the constraint will involve lower sales and/or growth. With the paid-out profits constraint, profits must be made, but the firm need not grow because retained profits may be zero.

A desire to maximize the present value of either profits or sales revenue accruing from the use of the firm's assets may result in growth. Growth is in these circumstances a means towards achieving another objective. A desire to maximize the growth rate of some aspect of the firm's operations itself is another possible objective. A number of variations of this objective are possible, depending upon whether the growth rate of paid-out profits, sales revenue, total assets, net assets, or some other aspect of the firm is to be maximized.

In the case of growth objectives, the desire to make profits is inherent in the objective itself, because profits are necessary in order to finance growth internally or to obtain additional outside finance. This applies whether the objective is to maximize the growth rate of profits, sales revenue, or net assets.

Decision makers may pursue other objectives which are variations on the theme of profit, sales revenue, or growth rate maximization. Instead of attempting to maximize sales revenue subject to a profit constraint a firm may, for example, wish to maximize profits subject to a self-imposed constraint in the form of a desire to achieve a certain level of sales revenue. The sales revenue constraint may be imposed by a desire on the part of the firm's management to prevent the firm's market share from falling in absolute or relative terms. Alternatively, the firm may wish to maximize profits or sales revenue subject to achieving a certain growth rate of the firm's net assets.

The nature of a firm's objectives is fundamentally important in influencing the characteristics of the firm's productive activities. It can be shown, for example, that the behavior of a firm confronted by a particular set of environmental conditions will differ depending upon whether the firm's objective is profit, sales revenue, or growth rate maximization. For the sake of simplicity the following exposition assumes that the funds available to the firm cannot be increased by resorting to outside finance; the reader is assured that the conclusions are not materially altered by dropping this assumption.

Consider, first, the behavior of a firm if the objective is to maximize the present value of profits resulting from the use of the firm's assets. The firm will produce a level of output which maximizes current profits. If all these profits are paid out to the firm's owners at the end of the first period, the stream of paid-out profits through time will consist of the same level of paid-out profits, repeated in each successive period, unless and until the firm's economic environment changes. Alternatively, the firm can retain some profits to finance growth of output and profits in each successive period. The firm can choose between lower paid-out profits in any period, growing at a faster rate through time, and larger paid-out profits in any period, growing at a slower rate through time. The problem of the firm with a profit-maximizing objective is to select a growth rate (implicitly in this model, a retention policy) which maximizes the present value of paid-out profits over the period to which the objective applies.

Consider next the behavior of the firm if the objective is to maximize the growth rate of output, sales revenue, profits, or some other variable. Growth requires funds to finance growth and, in this example, profits are the only possible source of finance for growth. Funds for growth, and the attainable growth rate, will be maximized if the firm produces a level of output which maximizes profits in the current period. Growth rate maximization and profit maximization (as defined above) lead to the same output decision in the current period. The growth rate maximizer will retain more profits than the profit maximizer; all profits over and above those needed to satisfy a minimum paid-out profit constraint will be used by the growth maximizer to finance growth. The level of output produced by the firm in any given future period will, it follows, be greater for a growth rate maximizer than for a profit maximizer, given the firm's economic environment.

Finally, consider the behavior of the firm if the objective is sales revenue maximization. Such a firm will produce a larger level of output than if the firm's objective were profit or growth rate maximization. In a single-period analysis, this proposition is explained by reference to the fact that a profit-maximizing level of output equates the marginal revenue and marginal cost of output, while a sales-revenue-maximizing level of output equates the marginal revenue to zero. Provided that the marginal cost of producing output is positive at all levels of output, a profit-maximizing level of output will be one involving positive marginal revenue, which in turn implies that total revenue can be increased by expanding output. A minimum-profit constraint sets a limit to the extent to which a firm can expand output beyond the profit-

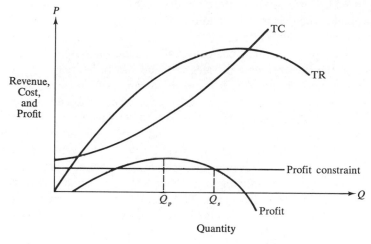

Figure 1-1 A Single-Period Constrained Sales Maximization Model

maximizing level. A single-period model of a firm maximizing sales revenue subject to a minimum profit constraint is shown in Figure 1-1. The firm's sales, or total revenue, is represented by curve TR, and its total costs by TC. Output Q_p maximizes the firm's current profit. At this output, the slope of the total cost curve (equals marginal cost) is equal to the slope of the total revenue curve (equals marginal revenue). However, since TR is still increasing (marginal revenue is positive) as output is increased, the firm expands output and produces and sells output Q_s, where further expansion of sales will decrease profits below a minimum acceptable level.

The reason why a firm whose objective is to maximize the *present value* of sales revenue will produce a larger output level than one whose objective is to maximize profits, is not immediately obvious. Why, it may be asked, should the firm deliberately sacrifice current profits, which can be used to finance increased future sales revenue, in order to expand current sales revenue beyond the profit-maximizing level? The explanation, in brief, is as follows: The present value of sales revenue depends upon the size of current sales revenue and the rate at which this level of sales revenue grows through time. The latter rate depends on the current profits of the firm, because these provide the means to finance growth of sales revenue in the future. Increasing the level of the firm's current output to the level which maximizes current profits increases both current sales revenue and the rate at which this revenue can grow through time, because this growth rate is determined by the profits retained after dividends have been paid and which are therefore available to finance growth of output and sales in the next period. At the level of output which maximizes current profits, sales revenue is still increasing (marginal revenue is positive and equal to marginal cost), but the maximum possible growth rate of sales revenue is constant, because this rate depends on profits, which are constant at such an output level. It follows that the present value of sales revenue can be increased by slightly increasing the level of output, because current sales revenue will be increased, yet the growth rate of sales revenue is not reduced. At levels of output larger than the profit-maximizing level, increasing the level of current sales revenue reduces profits and hence the attainable growth rate of sales revenue. In selecting an output level above the profit-maximizing level, the sales revenue maximizer must choose between larger current sales revenue, growing at a slower rate, and smaller current sales revenue growing at a faster rate. The combination of current sales revenue and growth rate which maximizes the present value of sales revenues must involve a level of output at which further increases in current sales revenue will reduce the growth rate of sales revenue through time. Since this growth rate will only fall if output is above the profit-maximizing level, the implication is that a maximizer of the present value of sales revenue will produce a larger output (in any particular period) than a profit maximizer.

The contrast between profit and sales-revenue maximization in a multiperiod setting can be further illuminated with the aid of Figure 1–2. The bottom half of the diagram, below the horizontal axis which represents levels of current sales revenue (hereafter abbreviated to S_c) is simply Figure 1–1 "turned on its side." In the top half of the diagram the vertical axis represents growth rate of current sales revenue (hereafter abbreviated to g). Curve OM depicts, for an individual firm, the maximum attainable g at different levels of S_c. As the level of current output and S_c are increased, profits and, because profits are required to finance growth, the maximum attainable g increase and reach a maximum at level of current sales S_p, then decline as sales are pushed beyond the level which maximizes current profits. Eventually, at a level of S_c involving zero profits, the maximum attainable growth rate is zero.

In order to demonstrate that a maximizer of the present value of sales

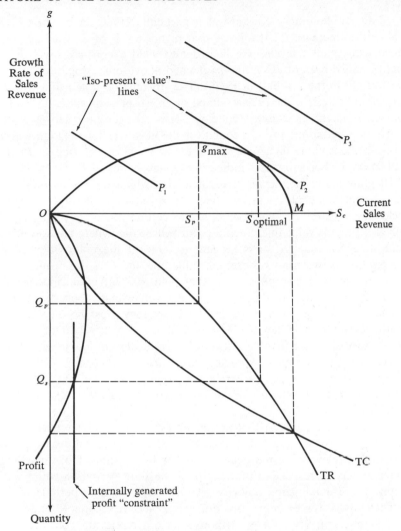

Figure 1–2 A Multiperiod Sales Maximization Model

revenue (hereafter abbreviated to P_s) will produce a larger scale of output than a profit (and growth rate) maximizer, it is necessary to introduce into the diagram "iso-present value" lines. It was pointed out earlier that, given the discount rate of the decision maker, the present value of sales revenue, P_s, depends upon both the level of current sales revenue and the growth rate of that revenue. An "iso-present value" line will be defined as the locus of combinations of S_c and g which (given the decision-maker's discount rate) yield a *constant* level of P_s. Holding S_c at any particular level, an increase in g will tend to increase

P_s; similarly, holding g constant at a particular level, an increase in S_c will tend to increase P_s. It follows that higher levels of S_c must be combined with smaller levels of g in order to yield a constant level of P_s; that is, an iso-present value line as defined above must slope down from left to right in the top half of Figure 1–2. It must be noted that without further information, the precise shape of an iso-present value line is not known; it might be convex, concave, or a straight line. However, all that is required in the present context is the negative slope. There will be an iso-present value line for every different value of P_s, such as P_1, P_2, and so on, higher subscripts indicating higher values of P_s.

Diagrammatically, the problem of a firm which desires to maximize the present value of sales revenue is to select a point on OM which yields the greatest P_s, which amounts to getting on to the highest possible iso-present value line. Such a point will be one where an iso-present value line just touches, or is tangent to, OM; if the point involved an intersection between an iso-present value line and OM this would automatically imply that a move to another point on OM could increase P_s. If, as has been argued above, iso-present value lines slope down from left to right, it follows that the point of tangency must lie on that portion of OM which is negatively sloped, that is, to the right of S_p. The point must therefore involve a level of current output and sales revenue larger than the profit-maximizing level. A profit (or growth rate) maximizer will, as argued earlier, select an output and sales revenue level which maximizes profits in the current period, that is, level Q_p and S_p in Figure 1–2.

It must be emphasized that any given objective, whether profit, sales revenue, or growth rate maximization, applies to a specific time period considered relevant by the decision maker in question. Objectives may differ merely in respect to the length of the time period to which they apply. Profit-maximizing objectives which apply to time periods of different lengths, for example, are different objectives, capable of leading to differences in behavior even though all other relevant considerations confronting the decision makers are the same.

It is appropriate at this point to consider in more detail the implications, for decision-makers' objectives, of the existence of uncertainty about the future. The profits anticipated in any future period as the result of a given pattern of behavior are not, in the presence of uncertainty, single-valued magnitudes. The decision-maker's estimate of profits anticipated in a future period may take the form of a probabilistic estimate, a range of possible values, each associated with a probability assigned by the decision maker himself, denoting the certainty with which the decision maker expects that particular outcome. In these circumstances, any particular objective, such as profit maximization, takes on new variations depending upon how "profits" are defined. Profits may, for example, refer to the mathematical expectation of profits, that is, to the sum of each possible outcome multiplied by its probability. Alternatively, the firm may be concerned with the dispersion of possible outcomes around this mean value, and may define relevant profits as the ratio of the mean expected profits to the dispersion of the possible outcomes around the mean. Or, alternatively, some other characteristic of the probability distribution of possible outcomes may be considered relevant by a decision maker. In these circumstances it cannot be argued that any particular measure of profits is more appropriate than another; the decision maker will adopt the measure he considers most appropriate, and behavior will be influenced by the measure chosen. The implications of uncertainty for objectives other than profit maximization, such as sales revenue or growth rate maximization, are similar. In each case, with uncertainty, a number of variations are possible depending upon which characteristics of the probability distribution of possible outcomes are considered an appropriate index of the variable to be maximized by the decision maker in question.

The preceding analysis has stressed that behavior depends upon the objectives pursued by decision makers, and that different objectives may imply differences in behavior.[3] It is appropriate at this stage to mention briefly possible similarities between behavior resulting from the pursuit of different objectives. A particular change in the economic environment may lead decision makers pursuing different objectives to respond in the same direction, if not to the same extent. The existence of a profit constraint in many firms' objectives may be responsible for such a situation; if profits are being sacrificed in order to achieve some objectives, an increase in costs will reduce profits below the level required to satisfy the constraint and cause the level of the firm's output to change in the same direction, *whatever* the objectives being pursued. In these circumstances it is impossible to infer the nature of the underlying objective simply from information on the direction of a response. Additional information is required for this purpose, and it becomes necessary to devise more elaborate operational tests to identify firms pursuing particular objectives. For example, an increase in a fixed cost—a cost which does not vary with the scale of a firm's output—will not cause a profit maximizer to change the level of his output. Because the total cost of producing any particular level of output is increased by the same amount, the slope of the total cost curve at any level of output (equals marginal

---

[3] The implications of the pursuit of objectives other than profit maximization for resource allocation in a general equilibrium setting are dealt with in Chapter Ten, in the section entitled Importance of Firms' Objectives.

cost) remains unchanged, and with it the profit-maximizing level of output. On the other hand, an increase in a fixed-cost item will cause a constrained sales revenue maximizer to reduce the scale of his output because the added costs will reduce profits at the old level of output below the minimum acceptable level. If the additional cost item varies with the scale of output, however, a profit maximizer will also change the scale of his output, increasing output if marginal cost at the old level of output is reduced, and reducing it if marginal cost at the old level of output is increased. If a firm is observed to change the scale of its output in response to a change in a fixed-cost item, the inference is that profit maximization is not the firm's objective, or possibly that the cost is not regarded as a fixed cost by the decision maker in question. As this example suggests, operational tests to identify firms pursuing particular objectives are difficult to devise, though not impossible.

For some purposes, it is not necessary to know the precise nature of the objectives pursued by firms responding in the same direction to a particular change in the economic environment. This is the case if one is interested only in predicting the direction of a response, instead of its precise magnitude, which usually requires precise knowledge of firms' objectives. In these circumstances, a single objective can be attributed to the decision makers in order to yield valid predictions concerning the direction in which they will respond to particular changes in their environment. The continued use of profit maximization as a basis for predicting firms' behavior may sometimes be justified on these grounds.

Optimum-Structured Firm

The size of the firm is a multidimensional concept including both stock and flow magnitudes. Dimensions of size include, for example, sales revenue, value added (sales minus purchases of raw materials, fuel and power), capital assets, number of employees, and other aspects of the firm's operations. A particular level of sales revenue is compatible with different levels of value added, reflecting differences in the vertical aspect of firm size, that is, the number of successive stages in the productive process performed by the firm. Specific levels of both sales revenue and value added are compatible with different degrees of diversification in terms of outputs, and also in terms of inputs combined in producing particular outputs. In what follows, the term "structure" is used in preference to "size," since it conveys better the fact that size is a multidimensional concept.

The optimum-structured firm is that structure of the firm which achieves certain objectives better than any other structure. Failure to distinguish a number of quite different concepts of the optimum-structured firm can lead to confused reasoning, and it must be stressed that the concept is entirely dependent upon the objective one has in mind. A firm with a particular structure may be optimal from the point of view of achieving one objective, and at the same time may be nonoptimal from the point of view of achieving a different objective. For example, what is optimal from the point of view of the decision maker controlling a firm, concerned perhaps with maximizing profits, need not be optimal from the point of view of public policy makers concerned with the allocation of the nation's resources. That is, a type and level of output which maximizes the firm's profits need not coincide with the type and level of output which makes the best use of the nation's resources.

From the point of view of the decision-making unit controlling the operations of a particular firm, the optimum-structured firm is a firm with characteristics which achieve the decision-maker's objectives better than any other structure. If one is interested in the determinants of a firm's behavior in practice, the objectives of the firm's decision-making unit are relevant, because actual structures will tend to reflect what the decision-making unit considers to be an optimal structure in the light of the decision-maker's economic environment.

In view of the possibility of different objectives when comparing different decision-making units, it is not surprising that different firms have different structures in practice even though the environmental conditions surrounding these firms are often very similar. If the objectives of different decision-making units differ, there is no such thing as "the" optimum-structured firm, valid for all firms.

It must be emphasized that, considering an individual firm, the optimum-structured firm may differ at different points in time, even though the decision-maker's objectives and environment remain unchanged. In all those situations in which achievement of the decision-maker's objective involves a positive rate of growth of some aspect of the firm's operations, the structure of the firm is determined by the point in its growth which it happens to have reached at a particular time. In these circumstances there is no optimum structure except at a point in time. Two firms which begin life at different points in time, each pursuing the same objective and operating in an identical environment, may continue to differ at any given point in time despite the pursuit of identical objectives and despite identical environmental conditions.

In much of the literature on price theory, the term "optimum-sized firm" refers to that level of a firm's output which minimizes the long-run average cost of producing the firm's product. This should not be interpreted to mean that, from a firm's point of view, the best scale of its operations is one which minimizes the unit cost of producing its product.

Only in the theoretical model of firm behavior which is designated perfect competition is this the case.

In the model of perfect competition, the demand curve confronting the individual firm is horizontal. Coupled with the assumption of freedom of entry into the industry, this results in a situation in which the profit-maximizing level of the individual firm's output is, in the long run, the level which minimizes the unit cost of producing the product. Producing a level of output which minimizes unit cost is, in these circumstances, a survival condition; only that level of output will yield the firm sufficient profits to induce the firm's decision makers to continue to produce that product.

In other market situations, the profit-maximizing level of a firm's output is not, in general, the level which minimizes the unit cost of the firm's product. This statement should not be misinterpreted. A firm will wish to minimize the total cost, and hence the average cost, of producing any particular level of output it decides to produce; it will not, however, necessarily decide to produce that level of output which minimizes the average cost of producing the product. The profitability of any given output level depends, in addition to average cost, on the anticipated price received per unit. This price may be different at different levels of the firm's output for it depends upon the firm's anticipations regarding the reactions of other firms in the same and in other industries, to its own output decision. In selecting its output level, the firm must have regard to the behavior of anticipated price received per unit, not only to cost per unit; the output level which maximizes profits will not necessarily be that level of output which minimizes the unit cost of producing the product. This distinction is referred to again in Chapter 3.

RECOMMENDED READINGS

1. Baldwin, W. L., "The Motives of Managers, Environmental Restraints, and the Theory of Managerial Enterprise," *Quarterly Journal of Economics,* May 1964.

2. Baumol, W. J., *Business Behavior, Value and Growth,* rev. ed. (New York: Harcourt, Brace & World, Inc., 1967).

3. ————, "On the Theory of Expansion of the Firm," *American Economic Review,* December 1962.

4. ————, *Economic Theory and Operations Analysis,* 2d ed. (Englewood Cliffs, N. J.: Prentice Hall, Inc., 1965), Chapter 19.

5. Cyert, R. M., and J. G. March, *A Behavioral Theory of the Firm* (Englewood Cliffs, N. J.: Prentice-Hall, Inc., 1963).

6. ————, and K. J. Cohen, *Theory of the Firm: Resource Allocation in*

a Market Economy (Englewood Cliffs, N. J.: Prentice-Hall, Inc., 1965), Part 3.

7. Machlup, F., "Theories of the Firm: Marginalist, Behavioral, Managerial," *American Economic Review,* March 1967.

8. McGuire, J. W., J. S. Y. Chiu, and A. O. Elbing, "Executive Incomes, Sales and Profits," *American Economic Review,* September 1962.

9. Mishan, E. J., "A Proposed Normalisation Procedure for Public Investment Criteria," *Economic Journal,* December 1967.

10. Simon, H. A., "Theories of Decision-Making in Economics and Behavioral Science," *American Economic Review,* June 1959.

11. ———, "New Developments in the Theory of the Firm," *American Economic Review,* Papers and Proceedings, May 1962.

12. Solomon, E., "The Arithmetic of Capital Budgeting Decisions," *Journal of Business,* April 1956.

13. Williamson, John, "Profit, Growth and Sales Maximization," *Economica,* February 1966.

14. Williamson, O. E., *The Economics of Discretionary Behavior: Managerial Objectives in a Theory of the Firm* (Englewood Cliffs, N. J.: Prentice-Hall, Inc., 1964).

CHAPTER TWO

INDUSTRY SUBGROUPINGS

Substitutability Criterion

For some purposes, such as international comparisons or comparisons within an economy at different points in time, one may be interested in the structure of industry as a whole, that is, in certain characteristics of the output of all firms in the economy taken together. In such cases the question of dividing firms into subgroups does not arise. For many other purposes, however, it is necessary to consider characteristics of the output of subgroups of firms in an economy. This is the case, for example, if one wishes to make interindustry comparisons of structure within a given economy, or between economies, at a point in time, or at different points in time. Indeed, the notion of subgroups of firms, termed "industries," is part of everyday life. When one attempts to define an "industry," however, matters are not so simple.

At first sight, the solution seems obvious, namely, to group together all those firms that produce the same product or service. This requires a definition of what constitutes the same product or service. Strictly, all firms produce different products because the products of two separate firms are produced at different geographical locations. Such a definition yields single-firm industries, and is too narrow for most purposes. At the other extreme, all products and services are the same in that they compete for consumers' purchasing power. Such a definition yields an economy-wide industry, and is too wide for most purposes.

There must be some aspect which is common to all firms in an industry, this much is clear. But there are many possible criteria for grouping firms into separate industries. Thus, one might group firms together according to common processes employed—printing, spinning, weaving, smelting. Alternatively, the grouping could be based upon the

17

use of common raw materials—cotton, iron and steel, wool. Again, one might group together firms producing a product with identical physical characteristics. It is clear that one is likely to get different groupings of firms depending upon whether the "same" product means physically identical, using the same process in its manufacture, or using the same inputs.

Economic theory indicates that, for a study of behavior, it is useful to define an industry as embracing those firms producing goods which are *close substitutes*. A measure of the degree of substitutability between two goods X and Y is provided by the concept of cross-elasticity of demand, defined as the ratio of the percentage change in the amount buyers demand of X to the percentage change in the price of Y which induces the change in the demand for X, the price of X and all other factors which are capable of influencing the demand for X being held constant. That is,

$$\text{cross-elasticity of demand} = \frac{\text{percentage change in the quantity of X demanded}}{\text{percentage change in the price of Y}}$$

If the sign of this expression is positive, the two goods are termed substitutes; if the sign is negative the two goods are termed complements. Provided that the sign is positive, the greater the proportionate change in quantity of X demanded when the price of Y changes by a given amount, the greater the degree of substitutability between the two goods.

The effect of a change in the price of Y on the quantity of X demanded, all other things remaining unchanged, can be hypothetically divided into an income effect and a substitution effect. If the numerator of the above expression is the sum of these two effects, one has a measure of gross cross-elasticity of demand accompanied by corresponding definitions of gross substitutes and complements. If, on the other hand, the numerator in the expression consists only of the substitution effect of a change in the price of Y on quantity of X demanded, one has a measure of net cross-elasticity of demand, with corresponding definitions of net substitutes and complements. The choice between these two definitions of cross-elasticity of demand can affect the resulting definition of the relationship between two goods. It is possible, for example, for two goods to be simultaneously gross complements and net substitutes. This would be the case if the substitution effect of a rise in the price of Y tends to increase the quantity of X demanded, but the income effect tends to reduce the quantity of X demanded and more than offsets the substitution effect. Alternatively, it is possible for two goods to be simultaneously gross substitutes and net complements. This would be the case if the substitution effect of a rise in the price of Y tends to reduce the quantity of X demanded, but X is an inferior good so that the income effect tends to increase the quantity of X demanded and more than offsets the substitution effect.

Cross-elasticity of demand measures substitutability on the demand side, that is, from the point of view of purchasers. A number of economists have stressed that the grouping together of firms into separate industries should also take into account substitutability on the supply side. This means that irrespective of the extent to which consumers consider the products of the individual firms to be substitutes, firms should be grouped together if the output of one firm is considered a close substitute for the output of another firm from the producer's point of view. For example, a firm producing only left-handed golf clubs would not be grouped with firms producing only right-handed clubs if the cross-elasticity of demand measure of substitutability were employed, because few buyers consider the two products to be close substitutes. The firms would be grouped together, however, using a measure of substitutability on the supply side, if one producer could easily switch his resources over to the production of the other firm's product in the event of a change in the price charged by the latter firm. Thus, one might measure substitutability on the supply side with a concept similar to cross-elasticity of demand, such as the ratio of the percentage change in the amount of X which producers of X would be willing to supply, to a percentage change in the price of Y, all other things remaining unchanged. Alternatively, some other measure of elasticity of technical substitution between different products might be employed.

Although the measures of cross-elasticity of demand and supply look similar, it must be emphasized that they differ; one refers to the response of potential buyers of X, and the other to the response of sellers of X, to a change in the price of Y, each response being measured in terms of the quantities of X demanded, and supplied, respectively. Neither of these measures, it should be added, necessarily reflects the change in the quantity of X *actually bought and sold*. This depends on the price of X, which is assumed to remain constant in calculating the cross-elasticity measures, and also on the possibility of nonprice responses by the producers of X.

Products can be operationally defined as substitutes or complements, and measures of the degree of substitutability obtained, only after empirical information has been obtained regarding the response of quantities demanded (or supplied) to changes in the price of other goods. Moreover, as already mentioned, it is necessary to add "all other things remaining the same" after the definition of cross-elasticities. There must be no change in the prices or in the nonprice variables, such

as level of advertising, for example, of other firms in response to a
change in the price charged by a particular firm for its product. Reflection on this point immediately suggests the difficulties likely to be
encountered in any attempt to obtain such information in practice. A
problem confronting the social scientist is that he is unable to "hold all
other things constant," and instead must rely upon statistical techniques
in an attempt to measure relationships such as cross-elasticities; these
techniques, however sophisticated, yield estimates of a probabilistic
nature.

Let us suppose, for the moment, that the required information could
be obtained easily. That is, one could obtain, for any particular firm's
product Y, a list of precise cross-elasticities (of demand, and also of
supply if considered appropriate) linking a change in the price of Y
to resulting changes in the demand for each other product in the economy. These could be ranked, commencing with large cross-elasticities
indicating a closer substitute relationship between Y and another product than between Y and products yielding smaller cross-elasticity
measures. A crucial problem remains. *Where* does one draw the line
between successive cross-elasticity magnitudes, thereby deciding which
goods are to be regarded as the "same" and which "different," and
therefore deciding also which firms are regarded as being members of
the "same" industry?

Economic theory provides no precise answer to this problem. There is
no magic value of cross-elasticity measures which divides "close" substitutes from "distant" substitutes. The choice of locating the dividing
line is a matter of opinion. A decision to draw the line where a definite
gap existed in the ranked cross-elasticity measures is just as arbitrary as
drawing the line elsewhere, from the point of view of theoretical justifi-
cation of such decisions.

In view of the difficulties of obtaining information about cross-elasticities, and the remaining element of arbitrariness involved in defining
industry boundaries even if the required empirical evidence were obtained without cost, is it possible to conclude that the substitutability
criterion is inferior, from a practical point of view, when compared
with other possible criteria such as similarity of technological process,
raw material, or physical characteristics? A negative answer to this
question is indicated if one investigates the reason why substitutability
is stressed in economics.

The rationale of the substitutability criterion is as follows. Economic
theory is largely concerned with the behavior of individual decision-
making units, such as firms. The behavior of any individual firm depends, among other things, on which other firms it takes into account
in its decision making. The firm's decision-making problem is to select

a set of values of the policy variables under its control, such as the price it charges, and the level of its investment in production, advertising, and R&D activities, which best achieves the firm's objective, such as profit maximization. If the profits which the firm expects to reap from a given set of policy variables is influenced by the activities of other firms, then the behavior of the firm depends also on the anticipated behavior of other firms.

All firms are likely to be affected in some degree by each others' actions. However, any particular decision maker is likely to confine his attention to only a few firms whose behavior he considers as a significant influence on the result of his own policies. The task, if one is interested in behavior, is to discover which firms take each others' behavior into account in deciding upon their own individual policies and to group them together accordingly, because the behavior of members of such a group will be related.

The use of cross-elasticity measures of substitutability is simply a method of discovering the degree to which firms are affected by each others' pricing behavior, in order to infer which firms are likely to take each other into account in deciding upon their individual policies. It should be emphasized that one could use some other measure of substitutability instead of cross-elasticity of demand; the response of the quantity of one firm's product demanded to a change in the level of another firm's advertising outlays, prices remaining constant, could be used, for example. Another point to bear in mind is that measures of substitutability, such as cross-elasticity of demand, refer to the extent to which one firm would lose or gain sales in response to a change in another firm's price, *assuming that the first firm did nothing in response to the price change*. This, and not the *actual* change in the quantity of the first firm's product demanded, which will depend upon the response of the firm to the price change, is the relevant measure if one is attempting to measure the degree of substitutability between products.

Of course, this increases the problems associated with any attempt to obtain measures of cross-elasticity, because reactions by firms producing close substitutes for the product of a firm initiating a price change are often likely to occur in practice. However, it is important to distinguish clearly between the use of cross-elasticity measures as an indicator of substitutability, and as an indicator of the type of behavior resulting from close substitutability. In the case of an industry composed of two firms selling an identical product, for example, the cross-elasticity of demand between the products of the two firms may be very large, yet, as indicated in the section of Chapter 4 entitled Importance of Assumed Reactions Rather than Numbers, the behavior of the rivals and the resulting price and production policies may take any of several forms.

Again, the value of cross-elasticity of demand between the products of different firms can be interpreted as being zero under both monopoly and pure competition, yet the behavior of firms in each of these two market situations is completely different and represents two extreme limiting cases in price theory. A price change by a firm under conditions of monopoly cannot affect the sales of other firms appreciably because by definition there are no close substitutes for the monopolist's product. In pure competition, a slight increase in price by one firm will remove that firm from the market, but this does not change the market price or demand for the output of any individual firm remaining in the market. Although a price cut by one firm will tend to attract all the buyers in the market and reduce sales of other firms to zero, some economists have argued that the rising marginal cost curves of individual sellers, which are essential to the existence of pure competition, limit the ability of any single seller to supply that demand, and that realizable cross-elasticity of demand between the products of two firms in pure competition is therefore zero. Professor E. H. Chamberlin, on the other hand, has argued that cross-elasticity of demand can be defined in a number of different ways, and that its value in pure competition can equal zero even without taking supply conditions into account.

The degree of substitutability, as measured by cross-elasticities which do not include allowance for competitive responses, is important in determining whether there is likely to be a reaction of any kind by other firms in response to a change in the (price) strategy of one firm; it cannot indicate what type of reaction is likely, however, nor the effect of a given move on the part of one firm on the behavior of firms producing close substitutes.[1]

Standard Industrial Classifications

Many countries, and some international organizations such as the United Nations, have their own standard industrial classifications which are used for purposes of official statistics concerning various aspects of the domestic, or world, economies. The 1968 revised edition of the United Kingdom Standard Industrial Classification, for example, consists of 27 Orders or major industrial groups as broad as Agriculture, Forestry, and Fishing; Mining and Quarrying; Food, Drink, and Tobacco; and so on. These in turn are divided into 181 subgroups, called Minimum List Headings. For example, within Order I, Agriculture, Forestry, and Fishing, the Minimum List Headings are as follows:

---

[1] Despite this, the literature dealing with attempts to classify behavior according to cross-elasticities is voluminous. In this connection see references (1)–(3) and (5)–(8) listed at the end of this chapter.

001   Agriculture and Horticulture
002   Forestry
003   Fishing

The Minimum List Headings are in turn broken down into further subdivisions. For example, within Minimum List Heading 001, Agriculture and Horticulture, there are three further subdivisions as follows:

001 1.   Farming and stock rearing
001 2.   Agricultural contracting
001 3.   Market gardening, fruit, flower, and seed growing

Similarly, the 1967 edition of the United States Standard Industrial Classification Manual lists ten alphabetical Divisions as follows:

Division A.   Agriculture, forestry, and fisheries
Division B.   Mining
Division C.   Contract construction
Division D.   Manufacturing
Division E.   Transportation, communication, electric, gas, and sanitary services
Division F.   Wholesale and retail trade
Division G.   Finance, insurance, and real estate
Division H.   Services
Division I.   Government
Division J.   Nonclassifiable establishments

Each Division is composed of a number of Major Groups each of which is assigned a two-digit number. For example, within Division A the Major Groups are as follows:

Major Group 01.   Agricultural production
Major Group 07.   Agricultural services and hunting and trapping
Major Group 08.   Forestry
Major Group 09.   Fisheries

Each Major Group is composed of a number of three-digit Industry Groups, each of which is further subdivided into a number of four-digit Industries. For example, Major Group 01, Agricultural production, is further subdivided as follows:

Group No.	Industry No.	
011		FIELD CROPS
	0112	Cotton
	0113	Cash grains
	0119	Field crops not elsewhere classified
012		FRUIT, TREE NUTS, AND VEGETABLES
	0122	Fruits and Tree Nuts
	0123	Vegetables
013		LIVESTOCK
	0132	Dairies
	0133	Broiler chickens
. . . .	. . . .	

In the United States SIC, the United States economy is divided into 99 Major Groups (designated by two-digit code numbers), subdivided into Industry Groups (three-digit code numbers) which are further divided into Industries (four-digit code numbers).

The standard industrial classifications used by individual countries differ from each other, making comparisons of data based upon domestic SICs impossible or at best hazardous. The United Nations Standard Industrial Classification (UNSIC) is the classification most frequently employed for comparisons of data relating to different countries. The 1958 revised edition of the UNSIC divides the whole field of economic activity into nine Divisions, each designated by a one-digit code number, except manufacturing which receives two one-digit numbers, as follows:

> Division 0   Agriculture, Forestry, Hunting, and Fishing
> Division 1   Mining and Quarrying
> Division 2–3 Manufacturing
> Division 4   Construction
> Division 5   Electricity, Gas, Water, and Sanitary Services
> Division 6   Commerce
> Division 7   Transport, Storage, and Communications
> Division 8   Services and Activities not adequately described

Each Division has ten subdivisions, called Major Groups. Each Major Group is identified by a two-digit number, the first digit indicating the Division and the first and second digits taken together identifying the Major Group of that Division. Each Major Group, in turn, can be subdivided into ten groups, each with a three-digit number. The UNSIC provides three levels of classification only, Divisions, Major Groups, and Groups, and is therefore less detailed than the British and American SICs which have, as already mentioned, four levels of classification. In the UNSIC, the activities corresponding to the four-digit codes of the United Kingdom and United States classifications are simply listed, without separate numbers, after the three-digit code number. Apart from the difference in detail provided, however, the UNSIC, consisting of 90 Major Groups and 900 Groups, is similar in principle to the United Kingdom and United States national classifications. In each case, for example, the units classified are establishments, and the principles of assigning establishments to industries are similar.

In all of the standard industrial classifications mentioned so far, primary emphasis in defining an industry is on the supply side of the economic picture. Most of the industries are defined in terms of establishments primarily engaging in producing a product or group of products that are related by technical process or raw materials used in their manufacture. The fact that the grouping is based mainly on similarity of technical process and/or raw materials involved does not necessarily mean that the grouping is inappropriate for a study of behavior. What we have referred to as substitutability on the supply side may well be related to similarity of process or raw materials. For example, one United States SIC industry (3312 Blast Furnaces, Steel Works, and Rolling Mills) includes firms producing steel strip, tar, tubing, wire, washers, and wheels. From the point of view of users, these products could hardly be claimed to be substitutes for each other, yet producers of the products may well regard them as substitutes on the supply side. Similarly, the fact that manufacturers of scarves, suspenders, and artificial flowers are grouped together in industry code 4494 of the United Kingdom classification could conceivably be justified on the grounds that the products are regarded as substitutes by the producers of such products. The behavior of such manufacturers could therefore be related even though the products are not regarded as close substitutes by consumers.

Although substitutability on the supply side is often important, substitutability on the demand side must also be considered if one is interested in the behavior of firms, and such considerations might suggest a different grouping to that based upon similarity of process or raw material only. Different raw materials or processes may be used to produce products which consumers consider to be very close substitutes. For example, in the United Kingdom SIC, makers of cloth, leather, and fur gloves are grouped into a different industry from makers of knitted gloves, yet intuition suggests that the behavior of such firms is likely to be related because of a high degree of substitutability on the demand side. Coke produced in beehive coke ovens is probably viewed by purchasers as a close substitute for coke produced as a by-product in petroleum refining and related industries, yet establishments producing these two types of coke are classified in different industries (code 3312 and 2911 respectively) in the United States SIC. Similarly, tin cans (U. S. Code 3411) and glass containers (U. S. code 3221) are close substitutes for many purposes but are found in two different Major Groups[2] in the United States SIC because of the different materials, process of manufacture, or types of machinery used in their manufacture, that is, differences in supply characteristics. Again, there may well be considerable competition between manufacturing industries and non-manufacturing industries; for example, the manufacture of canned fruits and vegetables (U.S. code 2033 and 2034) is closely competitive with the sale of fresh fruits and vegetables (U.S. code 0122 and 0123).

These examples demonstrate that consideration of demand substitut-

[2] The two Major Groups are, respectively, Fabricated Metal Products, (34) and Stone, Clay, Glass, and Concrete Products, (32).

ability often results in wider groupings than groupings based upon supply substitutability. On the other hand, the substitutability criterion will sometimes result in narrower groupings than those groupings resulting from strict adherence to similarity of a product's physical characteristics. Output has a geographical as well as a physical characteristic. Goods and services produced at widely separated geographical locations may be very poor substitutes from the point of view of both producers and consumers if the cost of transporting the product or consumer between these locations is high. Consumers of haircuts, for example, do not regard the services of all barbers in the country, or even in the same city, as nearly perfect substitutes for each other, and because of this the behavior of any particular local barber will only be influenced by, and influence in turn, the behavior of other barbers whose services have a similar geographical characteristic.

No single industrial classification could possibly suit all purposes, and criticism of existing standard industrial classifications on the grounds that they do not suit a particular purpose amounts to little more than arid argument concerning which aspect of industry is the most important. Behavior itself has many different aspects, and different groupings may be appropriate for a study of different aspects of firms' behavior. The important requirement which a standard industrial classification must fulfill is that it should be as complete and detailed as possible, in order that the information contained can be regrouped to suit the particular purpose of anyone wishing to use the data.

The units allocated to the different industries and trades identified by the United Kingdom and United States SIC are establishments (factories, farms, shops, mines) and not firms in the sense of a productive unit operating under the direction of a unified will, which may consist of more than one establishment. From a practical point of view, it is easier to identify an establishment than a firm in the above sense of the word. More important, however, is the fact that the more detailed the unit classified, the more detailed the industrial classification that can be attempted. Despite the wealth of detail provided in many existing official industry classifications—the 1967 edition of the United States SIC Manual exceeds 600 pages, for example—it can be argued that existing classifications do not provide sufficient detail concerning some aspects of industrial structure. For example, if an establishment produces more than one product according to the British and United States official product definitions, it is usually allocated to an industry on the basis of its major activity or primary product only. That is, an establishment is classified in a particular industry if the product of that industry accounts for a greater proportion of the total value of shipments from the establishment than any other product. For this reason, the number of establishments producing any particular type of output may be understated, the total output of a particular product may be understated or overstated, and information regarding the extent of diversification within establishments cannot be extracted from data based upon the SIC.

It is impossible to overemphasize the importance of the industry definition. If different criteria for grouping firms into separate industries result in different groupings, choice of criteria must influence the structural characteristics of the industries so defined unless the characteristics of different firms' output are identical, which is unlikely. This should always be remembered in appraising the results of any particular study of industrial structure.

It has been pointed out in the first section of this chapter that the appropriate classification of products and firms is one which reflects a high degree of substitutability, either on the demand or the supply side, between the products of individual firms. Ideally, the appropriate measures of substitutability would be cross-elasticities of demand and supply between different products. Unfortunately the data required to calculate such measures is seldom available, and we are restricted to more readily available indicators of substitutability. For example, two products can be considered to be substitutes on the supply side if they are commonly produced in the same establishments by essentially the same equipment, technical processes, and labor, and the proportions in which the products are produced can vary. The existing SIC emphasis on the technical structure of production is a reflection of this criterion. On the other hand, one would consider as distinct, on the supply side, two products found in the same establishment produced by distinct technical processes, or produced in rigid proportions by the same processes. On the demand side, those goods or services serving generally similar purposes, and among which buyers are frequently observed to vary the proportions of their purchases in response to price variations, can be considered substitutes.

Even if the data required to calculate precise measures of substitutability were available, it is doubtful whether such data would be worth the effort involved in obtaining it. The relationships between commodities are not fixed but change over time with changes in consumers' tastes, productive techniques, and the introduction of new products; therefore measures of the degree of substitutability between products, such as cross-elasticities of demand, may be expected to vary with the passage of time.

Provided that the substitutability criterion is kept in mind, it should be possible to avoid major errors in classifying products and firms into industries for a study of behavior. Thus, for example, it is fairly obvious that certain SIC groupings are too narrow; beet sugar (U.S. code 2063) and cane sugar (U.S. code 2061) four digit industries are too narrow, and the three digit classification (206—Sugar) is more appropriate if one is interested in the selling behavior of firms producing, respectively, beet sugar and cane sugar. Other groupings will be too wide, as in the case of products produced by firms at widely separated geographical locations and having a high transportation cost.

Although a priori reasoning and observance of the substitutability criterion may assist in grouping firms appropriately for a study of behavior, empirical studies are indispensable for deciding upon proper groupings, because only such studies can reveal which groupings are most closely related to whatever aspect of behavior one is interested in. Ideally, what is required, in order to decide which groupings are useful in explaining behavior, is that statistical studies investigating the relationship between various aspects of firms' behavior be repeated for different groupings of firms. Statistical evidence often shows broadly similar results for studies using different classifications of firms into industries; of course, this does not necessarily imply that groupings are irrelevant, or that the particular groupings used were the most appropriate—they may be equally inappropriate. However, by investigating whether and how different industry classifications influence the results of statistical studies, it may be possible to improve upon existing knowledge of which groupings are significant from a behavioral point of view.

RECOMMENDED READINGS

1. Bishop, R. L., "Elasticities, Cross-Elasticities, and Market Relationships," *American Economic Review*, December 1952; comments by W. Fellner and E. H. Chamberlin, and reply by Bishop, *American Economic Review*, December 1953, pp. 898–924; comment by R. Hieser, and reply by Bishop, *American Economic Review*, June 1955, pp. 373–386.
2. ———, "Market Classification Again," *Southern Economic Journal*, July 1961.
3. Chamberlin, E. H., *Towards a More General Theory of Value* (New York Oxford University Press, 1957) pp. 84–91.
4. Conklin, M. R., and H. T. Goldstein, "Census Principles of Industry and Product Classification, Manufacturing Industries," in G. J. Stigler (ed.), *Business Concentration and Price Policy* (Princeton, N. J.: Princeton University Press, 1955).
5. Heertje, A., "Market Classification Systems in Theory," *Southern Economic Journal*, October 1960.
6. Pfouts, R. W., and C. E. Ferguson, "Market Classification Systems in Theory and Policy," *Southern Economic Journal*, October 1959.
7. ———, "Conjectural Behavior Classification of Oligopoly Situations," *Southern Economic Journal*, October 1960.

8. ———, "Theory, Operationalism, and Policy: A Further Note on Market Classification," *Southern Economic Journal,* July 1961.

9. United Nations, *International Standard Industrial Classification of all Economic Activities,* Statistical Papers, Series M, No. 4, Rev. 1. (New York: Statistical Office of the United Nations, 1958).

10. United Kingdom Central Statistical Office, *Standard Industrial Classification,* 3d. ed. (London: Her Majesty's Stationery Office, 1968).

11. United States Bureau of the Budget, *Standard Industrial Classification Manual* (Washington, D.C.: U.S. Government Printing Office, 1967).

CHAPTER THREE

COST CONDITIONS

Short-Run Versus Long-Run Cost Conditions

The term cost conditions refers to the relationship between different levels of a firm's output of a particular product or service and the cost of producing and distributing that product or service. It is customary to distinguish three concepts of cost: total cost, average cost, and marginal cost. Average cost is simply the total cost of any level of output divided by the number of units of output produced. Marginal, or incremental cost, is the change in total cost associated with a change in the level of output. Diagrammatically, plotting total cost vertically and level of output horizontally, marginal cost is the slope of the total cost curve at a particular output level.

The costs of producing and distributing any product are simply the sum of the costs of the various inputs used. It is assumed that the inputs used in the production and distribution of a particular product are combined in a manner which minimizes the total cost of producing and distributing any particular level of output in the light of existing knowledge concerning production methods.

A distinction is drawn in economic theory between short-run and long-run cost conditions. Short-run cost conditions describe the relation between different levels of output of a particular product and the costs of producing the product in a situation in which the decision maker, whose objective is to minimize the total cost of producing any particular level of output, is confronted by a constraint which does not exist in the long run. Specifically, short run refers to a period of time during which the amount of at least one of the inputs combined in the production of the product cannot be varied, whereas long run refers to a period of time during which the decision maker is free to vary all inputs as he wishes.

The U-shaped short-run average and marginal cost curves of elementary economic theory result from the assumption of first increasing then eventually diminishing marginal physical productivity of variable inputs when combined with a fixed input. The U shape of the curve may be accentuated by increases in the price of variable inputs as the quantity purchased by the firm is increased.

Whether short-run cost curves are U shaped in practice can only be ascertained by empirical investigation. Evidence concerning the shape of short-run cost curves suggests that while average variable cost decreases at first in some industries, in many other industries the average variable cost curve is approximately horizontal, up to a level of output associated with the capacity output of the fixed input in question, followed by sharply increasing unit costs. The conditions resulting in such observations need not always correspond to the assumptions made in elementary price theory, namely that a fixed input is being combined with increased amounts of variable input, and that the state of technological knowledge confronting all firms is the same. The services of fixed capital equipment may, for example, be variable so that the amount of fixed input per unit of variable input is not in fact being decreased. More will be said later concerning the problems associated with estimating cost conditions.

Economies and Diseconomies of Scale

In the long run, all inputs used in the production and distribution of a particular product can by definition be varied, and the relationship between cost of production and level of a firm's output is governed by what are termed economies and diseconomies of scale. These terms are applied, respectively, to factors which cause long-run average cost (hereafter referred to as LRAC) to decline, or to increase, as the total output of a particular product or service increases. It should be noted that the state of knowledge concerning production methods is assumed to be unchanged in long-run analysis; however, this does not necessarily mean that the methods of production employed by a firm will be the same at different levels of output.

Simple geometric relationships between the material required for the construction of certain items of equipment and the equipment's capacity may account for declining long-run average costs as the level of output of some products increases. The amount of material required for constructing containers, for example, depends mainly upon the surface area of the container, whereas the capacity of the container depends on the volume enclosed. A storage tank is perfectly divisible in the sense that it can be built to any particular size specifications. However, the capacity of a storage tank will increase more than proportionately with increases in its surface area, and if the cost of the tank is proportional to surface area, unit storage costs will decline as tanks of larger and larger size are employed. Again, if a particular productive process requires liquid to be kept at a certain temperature, and heat loss is proportional to the surface area of the tank containing the liquid, the cost of keeping a unit of the liquid at a certain temperature will decline as the size of the tank is increased, because the cost of compensating for heat loss will increase less than in proportion to the capacity of the container. Another example of geometric relationships as a source of economies of scale concerns pipes; the capacity of a pipe depends on the cross-sectional area of the pipe, which increases more than proportionately with increases in the pipe's circumference—the chief determinant of material requirements used in the pipe's construction. Apart from the economies of scale arising in circumstances in which an increase in capacity and output does not require a porportionate increase in material, the labor cost of constructing or installing items of fixed equipment often varies with the amount of material being worked, rather than with capacity of the equipment being installed. Therefore, these geometric relationships often save labor costs in addition to material costs.

It must be stressed that merely increasing the physical size of items of equipment does not inevitably lead to falling unit costs. Larger dimensions of a storage tank or pipeline may, for example, require stronger materials. Alternatively, a larger ship may require larger engines, and after some size is reached reductions in unit carrying costs attributable to larger dimensions may be offset by increased fuel costs per unit carried.

Apart from geometric relationships, a second source of economies of scale arises from the fact that some inputs are indivisible below a certain size. Some items of capital equipment required to perform certain operations, for example, do not come in small sizes. Up to the capacity output of minimum-sized indivisible inputs, the cost of these inputs per unit of output produced will fall as scale of output increases, and therefore LRAC will decline with increases in scale of output, assuming, of course, that other input costs per unit of output are constant, or do not increase sufficiently to increase the total unit cost of larger scales of output.

The influence of indivisibility of machinery on unit costs may be magnified where balancing of processes is involved. Suppose, for example, that production of a particular product involves three different processes performed respectively by indivisible machines with a capacity output of 1000, 500, and 750 units. Cost per unit of final product is minimized when 3000 units of output (or any multiple of this amount) are produced; this equals the least common denominator of the capacity outputs of each of the three machines. 3000 units of output requires 3, 6, and 4 machines respectively working at full capacity. At any smaller output level, the unit cost of producing the final product will be greater because at least one type of machine will be operating at less than capacity level.

Indivisibility of inputs is not confined to items of capital equipment. Human inputs may account for economies of scale. A manager may be able to supervise production of 1000 units of output as easily as 500. The fact that, up to a point, his salary is spread over more and more units of output is by itself not sufficient to explain declining *long-run* average cost; in addition, the managerial input must be indivisible in the sense that it is impossible to acquire a *different* manager to supervise smaller levels of output at proportionately lower salary than that paid to managers supervising larger output levels.

Another type of indivisibility which may result in declining LRAC with increases in scale of output concerns the division of labor. If, for example, two men produce more output when each specializes in one process than when both perform both tasks, the unit cost of output will be higher when total output produced is not sufficient to require the services of more than one man working full time. Unit costs would only remain constant if it were possible to hire two men, each working half time.

There are other examples of economies of scale. Whenever set-up costs are involved in a particular productive operation, such as fixing a die in a press, the set-up cost per unit of output diminishes with increases in the scale of output. In addition, longer production runs often make it possible to reduce unit costs by automating production and substituting capital for labor. Finally, optimal inventory levels are likely to increase less than proportionately with increases in the scale of a firm's output, resulting in a reduction in inventory cost per unit of output. The principle underlying so-called "stochastic economies of scale" associated with inventories can be explained briefly, using the example of spare components kept on hand to take care of possible machinery breakdowns, as follows. Optimal component inventory levels per unit of output depend upon two characteristics of the probability distribution of expected component failures per unit of output: the mean probable number of failures per unit of output, and the variance of the expected number of failures per unit of output. If the failure of one component is independent of other such failures, then as scale of output increases and capacity is increased through duplication of machinery, the mean number of expected failures per unit of output remains unchanged, but the variance of expected failures per unit of output declines. Therefore, the optimum inventory of spare components per unit of capacity and output will decrease. The principle also applies to inventory levels of work-in-progress and finished goods kept, respectively, to meet random work-flow stoppages or variations in demand. Stochastic economies of scale can also apply to the size of the stand-by labor force needed to repair breakdowns in machinery and equipment.

The level of output at which unit costs are minimized is sometimes referred to as the minimal optimal scale of output. This terminology, as mentioned in Chapter 1, should not be interpreted to mean that the producer's objective is always to minimize the unit cost of producing and distributing his product. This objective only becomes a condition of survival in a purely competitive market, for in such a case the level of output which minimizes unit costs also maximizes (long-run) profits. In other market situations, however, unit cost minimization may conflict with the decision maker's objectives. In Figure 3–1, for example, assuming that the decision maker's objective is profit maximization, the optimal level of output is Q_1, which differs from the (average) cost-minimizing level of output Q_2.

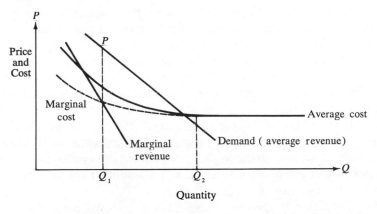

Figure 3–1   Profit Maximizing versus Average Cost Minimizing Levels of Output

The empirical evidence contained in a number of studies listed at the end of this chapter suggests that there are economies of scale in the production of many goods and services, leading to a downward-sloping LRAC curve at low levels of output.

Turning now to diseconomies of scale, a number of hypotheses have been put forward purporting to explain why LRAC curves must eventually turn up. If, as a firm expands the scale of its output, the price which it must pay per unit of one or more of the inputs used by the firm increases, the unit cost of its output may increase; that is, rising input supply curves may be responsible for an upturn in the firm's LRAC curve.

A second class of argument involves the concept of managerial diseconomies of scale. In this context, it is not sufficient to point out that there is a physical limit to what a manager (or a fixed team of managers) can do. This may be relevant to explaining why short-run average cost curves turn up after some scale of output is reached, but in order to explain why long-run average cost curves turn up because of managerial diseconomies, it is necessary to explain why, for example, a proportionate increase in the scale of all inputs *including managerial inputs* causes the firm's total costs to increase more than in proportion to output.

One prominent explanation of why this may occur involves the concept of control loss.[1] In all but the very smallest business organizations, the information upon which the top executive, or peak coordinator, must base his decisions, and the instructions based upon this information, must be transmitted across successive hierarchical levels. Such transmission results in a serial reproduction loss, or distortion, of the information and instructions, even though the objectives of people forming successive links in the hierarchical chain may not conflict in any way. Increasing the scale of a firm's output will increase the number of hierarchical levels over which information and instructions must pass, which exposes the data to further distortion and therefore results in a reduction in the *quality* of both the information reaching the peak coordinator and the instructions passed down to operating personnel. In addition, since the capacity of the peak coordinator for assimilating information and issuing instructions is limited, he can only acquire the additional information and issue the additional instructions, necessitated by an expansion in the scale of the firm's operations, by sacrificing some of the detail provided before the expansion (assuming he was initially fully employed). That is, the *quantity* of information received and transmitted per unit of output will be less after expansion than before.

This reduction in quality of data provided to the peak coordinator and in quality of instructions supplied to operating units made necessary by an expansion in the scale of a firm's output is referred to as control loss. Because of this phenomenon, it may be argued that the behavior of a firm's operating units will not correspond as closely to the peak coordinator's objective of minimizing costs as it did prior to expansion of the scale of a firm's output, resulting in an increase in the firm's unit costs as the scale of output is increased.

---

[1] See O. E. Williamson "Hierarchical Control & Optimum Firm Size," *Journal of Political Economy*, April 1967, reference (13).

The reader is reminded that economies and diseconomies of scale refer to the behavior of unit costs in a given state of technological knowledge. A tendency for unit costs to rise as the result of control loss experienced as firms expand the scale of their output may be partially or totally offset by new technological developments which widen the information-processing capability and span of control of the firm's peak coordinator or his subordinates. That is, static limits to firm size may be constantly receding with the passage of time as new knowledge results in improvements in ability to coordinate and control the operations of large-scale enterprises.

Another class of arguments focuses upon uncertainty as a factor causing the LRAC curve associated with a firm's product to turn up after some scale of output is reached. If one of the functions of management is that of adjusting a firm's operations to unpredictable variations in the demand and cost conditions confronting the firm, then the existence of any degree of uncertainty confronting a firm will give rise to the need for management and therefore cause the firm's LRAC curve to turn up due to the control loss phenomenon discussed in the preceding paragraphs. It is also undoubtedly true that the greater the degree of uncertainty regarding changes in conditions confronting a firm, the greater are likely to be the costs of dealing with uncertainty associated with gathering and organizing information concerning the firm's economic environment and making decisions which provide the appropriate instructions to subordinates. That is, more information will be required by management to assist in the detection of changes in conditions, and more frequent decisions will be required, as the degree of uncertainty confronting a firm increases. This is not, however, the same as saying that uncertainty causes increasing unit costs with increases in the scale of a firm's output; it merely explains why the cost of producing a particular level of output will be higher, the greater the degree of uncertainty confronting the firm producing the output. A crucial question is whether the degree of uncertainty itself is likely to vary with increases in the scale of a firm's output, either increasing and causing the LRAC curve to turn up earlier than it would do otherwise as a result of the control loss phenomenon, or decreasing and therefore postponing or offsetting the tendency for LRAC to turn up because of control loss. Fluctuations in the demand or cost conditions confronting an individual firm operating in a particular industry may result from changes in the demand or cost conditions confronting the industry as a whole, caused by influences external to the industry; alternatively, such fluctuations may occur because of changes in the behavior of the firm's rivals in the industry, even though the demand and cost conditions confronting the industry as a whole are unchanged. It can be argued that the degree of uncertainty associated with the activities of a firm's rivals in the industry will be smaller, the larger the proportion of industry output supplied by the firm and the smaller the number of rivals in the industry. Under conditions of monopoly, for example, this source of uncertainty will be completely absent. On the other hand, the larger the firm's output, relative to industry output, the greater will be the absolute impact on the firm of a change in the industry demand or cost conditions, and from this point of view it can therefore be argued that the degree of uncertainty confronting a firm increases as the scale of the firm's output increases. As this example indicates, purely a priori arguments concerning the relationship between the scale of a firm's output and the degree of uncertainty confronting the firm are rather inconclusive.

Empirical evidence accumulated thus far seems to be inconsistent, with an upturn in the LRAC curve associated with the product of most industries. There may be no upturn, or it may occur at a larger output level than that achieved by firms in practice. There is, as yet, no general agreement among economists as to whether the empirical evidence is consistent with constant costs (above a certain minimum scale of output) or continually declining LRAC. The reasons for disagreement concerning these matters revolve around problems encountered when an attempt is made to estimate cost conditions existing in various industries in practice. These matters will be treated further in the sections entitled Estimating Cost Conditions, and Growth Rates and Cost Conditions.

Cost Conditions and Other Structural Features

Cost conditions influence a number of other features of industrial structure.

The level of a firm's output of a particular product is influenced *directly* by the nature of the cost conditions associated with producing and distributing that product. Given the demand conditions confronting the firm, and the firm's objectives, cost conditions determine how much output the firm will produce.

The question of whether the LRAC curve associated with a particular product turns up after some scale of output has been reached is intimately bound up with the question of whether there exists some limit to the size of individual firms. If there are no diseconomies of scale in producing individual products, there is nothing to prevent a firm from expanding until it supplies the total market for an individual product. Downward-sloping market demand curves for individual products will impose a limit upon the size of a firm's operations in any individual market; that is, it will become unprofitable to expand the scale of the firm's output beyond a certain level since price will ultimately fall below unit cost. Since firms are not, however, restricted to the sale of a single product, but can diversify and expand by producing other products, downward-sloping market demand curves alone cannot impose a limit upon the firm's size. Total revenue will expand at the same rate as output provided that the firm is not forced to cut its prices in individual markets in order to expand. Only if the firm's total costs increase at a faster rate than output—that is, if there are diseconomies of scale—will there be a limit to the size of the firm in the long run. It must be added that even in the absence of diseconomies of scale there may be a limit to firm size at any point in time, a limit imposed by the need to obtain funds for expansion, combined with a limitation on the supply of funds available to the firm in any subperiod. That is, the need for capital to finance expansion may set a limit to the size of the firm at any given point in time, even in the absence of diseconomies of scale, but there will be no limit in the long run unless diseconomies of scale exist.

Economies and diseconomies of scale help determine whether there are few or many firms producing a particular kind of output, that is, the degree of seller concentration in a particular industry. Given industry demand conditions for a particular product, if existing firms in the industry compete on a price basis, only the firms with unit costs below industry price can survive; if unit costs depend upon scale of output, the number of firms in the industry will therefore be influenced by economies and diseconomies of scale. If firms compete on a nonprice basis, through advertising, style changes, or other strategies, this shifts up the unit cost curves of all firms and, given industry price, economies and diseconomies of scale will, again, influence the number of firms producing the total industry output demanded at a particular price.

Cost conditions may also influence the level of the firm's output *indirectly,* by influencing entry barriers into the firm's industry and hence demand conditions confronting the group of firms established in the industry. The demand conditions for a firm's product depend upon the reactions of firms already established in the industry and potential entrants into the industry. As will be explained in Chapter 7, entry barriers, which influence the behavior of potential entrants, depend to a large extent upon cost conditions associated with the product of the industry.

Finally, the degree of diversification in a firm, or industry, is influenced by the cost conditions governing the production of individual types of output, as explained in Chapter 9.

Estimating Cost Conditions

There are three main methods of attempting to estimate the cost conditions associated with the production of a particular type of product or service. These methods attempt to answer the following question. Given the state of technology and knowledge, how do costs of producing a given product vary with the level of output? First, there is statistical cost analysis, which uses information regarding the actual cost of producing output in firms producing different levels of the output in question. Second, the technological studies or engineering estimates method uses estimates of what the costs of producing different levels of output would be, even though these output levels are not in fact being produced. The third method, the survival technique, employs data on shares of industry output contributed by different-sized firms in order to infer the shape of the cost curve.[2]

The method used will often be dictated by the information available. Thus, for example, the first method requires a reasonably large number of firms producing the product in question while the third method requires at least two firms, and if these requirements are not satisfied, method two is the only alternative available.

The first method encounters problems associated with the valuation of fixed capital assets. The outlay on these inputs, which is a cost of production, is by convention spread over a number of periods in the firm's accounts. Even though different firms use identical capital equipment, the capital input cost figure in any accounting period may reflect differences in the depreciation methods used by different firms. Not only the methods used, but the time period over which the cost of equipment is spread, may differ from firm to firm, reflecting differences in estimates of how long the equipment will last physically or economically, and therefore in the appropriate period over which the cost should be spread. The relevant consideration, if one is concerned with estimating the *long-run* average cost of producing a product, is the cost of new equipment embodying the most efficient known methods of production, not the cost of old equipment. The capital equipment used by firms in an industry may not represent the most efficient known methods of producing a particular level of output. This might result, for example,

---

[2] Examples of studies employing these three methods of estimation are listed at the end of the chapter. Thus, the Johnston (6) reference deals with the statistical cost method, while the Bain (2) and Haldi (3) references deal with the technological studies method. The Saving (7), Shepherd (9), Stigler (11), and Weiss (12) references are concerned with the survival technique.

from different firms entering the industry at different historical points in time when technical knowledge differed. In these circumstances, statistical cost analysis will not yield an estimate of the relationship between unit cost and scale of output *using the most efficient known methods.*

Even if firms use the same depreciation methods and their equipment embodies the latest technological knowledge, firms may be producing scales of output with capital equipment which does not minimize the long-run average cost of producing those output levels. That is, a firm may be in a position of short-run equilibrium only, waiting for its existing equipment to wear out before replacing the equipment with equipment that will reduce the cost of producing its existing level of output. In these circumstances, statistical cost analysis will confuse short-run with long-run average cost conditions. This is perhaps the most serious deficiency of the statistical cost study method; cross-section data concerning the cost of producing a particular kind of output in different sized firms will inevitably reflect short-run costs unless every firm in the industry is in a position of long-run equilibrium. The requirement that all firms be in a position of long-run equilibrium will hardly ever be satisfied in practice. In addition, one cannot assume that the observed short-run costs of producing a particular level of output in a large number of firms of equal size will be evenly distributed around the long-run cost of producing that output level. This will in fact be impossible, because it follows from the definition of long-run cost that the short-run cost of producing a particular output level can exceed but cannot possibly be less than the long-run cost of producing that output level.

The second method of estimating cost conditions, the technological studies method, is sometimes criticized on the grounds that the cost figures obtained by using this method are hypothetical. However, if one is interested in knowing what the cost of output levels which differ from the one currently being produced would be (and such information is indispensable to optimizing behavior, that is, knowing whether one can achieve one's objectives any better) that is precisely the information required by the decision maker. It is not the hypothetical nature of the data that is to be criticized; rather, the difficulty of obtaining *accurate* hypothetical information, particularly estimates of distribution and other nonproduction costs.

The first and second methods of estimating cost conditions are complicated by the presence of multiproduct firms, that is, firms which produce a number of different products. In such cases, the cost of inputs that are used to produce more than one product must be apportioned between the products in order to provide an estimate of the cost of individual products. As with a single-product firm, the relevant cost to a multiproduct firm of one product is its marginal cost; however, accounting cost data is often based upon a more or less arbitrary allocation which does not reflect marginal cost accurately.

The third method, referred to as the survivor or survival technique, proceeds to estimate the shape of the long-run average cost curve for the product of a particular industry in the following manner. The firms in an industry are grouped into size classes, and the share of industry output (or some other index of size) accounted for by each size class at two or more points in time is compared. The shape of the long-run cost curve is inferred by assuming that changes in the share of industry output of any size class are related to the average cost of producing and distributing the product in that size class. Size classes experiencing an increase in the share of industry output are assumed to have minimum average costs. Size classes experiencing a declining share of industry output are assumed to be relatively inefficient, that is, are assumed to have higher unit costs. It has been further assumed in some studies employing this technique that the more rapid the rate at which a size class loses it share of the industry's output, the higher the unit cost of production in that size class relative to the cost of production in firms whose share is increasing. It does not necessarily follow, however, that those sizes which are experiencing a falling share of industry output have higher costs than those firms experiencing increases in share. Firms experiencing reductions in the share of industry output may be just as efficient but may face slightly different economic environments which prevent them from growing as rapidly as other firms; alternatively, the objectives of such firms may involve lower growth rates than other firms having the same unit costs.

The fundamental postulate of the survival principle is that competition between different-sized firms sifts out the more efficient enterprises, and that the firms which survive best will be those operating at lower average costs. It is essential, therefore, that firms used in a study employing the survival principle be competing in the same market; otherwise, the eliminating mechanism will be absent. There must be no barriers, based upon spatial distance or product differentiation, which prevent competition. Also, the technique may not yield an accurate estimate of the shape of the LRAC curve if there are factors dampening the elimination process, such as price agreements or collusive agreements to restrain competition.

The survival technique can indicate only the shape of the LRAC curve, showing the size of firm, or range of firm sizes, where cost per unit of output is lowest; it cannot, as can the other two methods, indicate the precise level of unit money cost at any particular scale of output.

Although the survival technique has been used to yield an estimate of the shape of the LRAC curve in certain industries, it must be emphasized that unless technology has remained constant over the period to which the study refers, such an interpretation of the results may be invalid. Rather than reflect relative efficiency in the static sense of the average cost of producing different levels of output in an environment in which technological information is the same for all firms, the technique may instead reflect the relative efficiency of different-sized firms in producing and in taking advantage of new knowledge. Unit costs may be lower, and the share of industry output may be growing faster, because firms of a certain size are more efficient in producing and using new knowledge. For example, it is possible to visualize circumstances in which there are no economies of scale in the static sense of lower unit cost at larger scale of output, yet in which the survival technique will yield an L shaped cost function, indicating that, up to a certain size, larger firms are more efficient in the use of resources to add to knowledge, improve products, and reduce costs through technical innovation.

Growth Rates and Cost Conditions

A number of economists have attempted to infer the shape of the long-run average cost curve associated with individual products from information about the growth rates of different-sized firms.[3] Under this approach, firms in an industry are grouped into size classes according to some index of size, such as assets, the growth rate of each firm's assets over a specified period of time is calculated, and the shape of the long-run average cost curve is inferred by assuming that the average growth rate of firms in each size class and unit costs in that size class are inversely related.

Before proceeding to outline the evidence revealed by this approach, it is appropriate to consider the rationale of such a method. In what circumstances do larger growth rates indicate lower unit cost? At any level of industry price, the profit rate on capital investment will be greater for firms with lower unit cost. Growth of a firm's operations requires funds to finance expansion, and profits largely determine the amount of funds available for expansion because profits are necessary either to finance expansion internally or to obtain outside finance. Therefore, the maximum attainable growth rate will be related to the profit rate, which, given industry price, depends upon unit cost.

---

[3] See, for example, reference (5), S. Hymer and P. Pashigian, "Firm Size and Rate of Growth," *Journal of Political Economy*, December 1962.

Although maximum attainable growth rates will be related to the height of unit cost, it does not necessarily follow that actual growth rates will be so related. Even if their unit costs are the same, firms with different objectives may grow at different rates, as explained in Chapter 1. That is, differences in actual growth rates between firms may reflect different objectives rather than differences in unit cost. Therefore, if the objectives of different-sized firms are different, their growth rates need not reflect differences in the unit cost of production. It is not essential, if relative growth rates of different-sized firms are to reflect differences in unit cost, that all firms aim at growth maximization; what does seem to be required is that firms of different sizes pursue the same objective, which may be maximization of either growth, profits, sales revenue, or some other variable. This is a strict requirement indeed, and one might well doubt whether it is likely to be satisfied in practice. However, even though different firms in any size class pursue different objectives, provided that the objectives resemble those pursued by firms in any other size class, the average growth rates of different-sized firms may tend to reflect differences in unit cost rather than differences in objectives.

A considerable amount of empirical evidence[4] suggests that there is no difference between the average growth rates of different-sized firms. Some economists have argued that such evidence is inconsistent with the existence of diseconomies of scale. If there were diseconomies of scale, expansion of a firm beyond a certain size in a given market would lead to higher unit cost and lower profit margins. The large firms in an industry would grow more slowly than small firms in the industry. The evidence suggests that this does not happen, hence the inference is that diseconomies of scale do not exist, at least up to the scales of output reached by firms in practice.

There is disagreement among economists as to whether the statistical evidence regarding average growth rates is consistent with constant or continually declining unit costs as scale of output increases. It must be emphasized that the constant cost hypothesis is not that costs are constant at all levels of output; proponents of the hypothesis acknowledge that economies of scale exist at low levels of output in many, if not most, industries. The question at issue is whether, beyond some minimum scale of output, unit costs are constant or continue to decline as scale of output increases.

The argument that the existence of similar average growth rates for

---

[4] See S. Hymer and P. Pashigian, reference (5); also A. Singh and G. Whittington, reference (10). See also, H. A. Simon and C. P. Bonini, "The Size Distribution of Business Firms," *American Economic Review,* September 1958; P. E. Hart and S. J. Prais, "The Analysis of Business Concentration," *Journal of the Royal Statistical Society,* 1956.

different-sized firms implies constant unit costs, at least beyond some minimum scale of output, has been challenged by the following argument.[5] If cost curves are continually falling, smaller firms in an industry will have smaller unit profits and will tend to be driven out of the industry. On the other hand small firms will have an incentive to expand and realize economies of scale. The small firm has, it is argued, a greater probability of decline because of high unit costs than does the large firm, and at the same time a greater probability of faster growth because of the incentive to realize cost savings through increased size. Therefore, it is claimed, the dispersion in growth rates should be higher for small firms than large firms, but there is no reason why the average growth rates should differ.

It is appropriate to mention several points concerning the logic of the preceding argument. First, it is not entirely clear why the incentive to expand should be greater for small than for large firms, if costs are continually declining as hypothesized. Why, if unit costs can be reduced by expanding further, should large firms have less incentive to expand than smaller firms? Second, the argument seems to deny the dependence of growth upon profits; even if the incentive to expand is greater for small firms than large, profit rates and therefore the *means* to grow, in the form of internal funds or additional external finance, will be smaller in the case of small firms, preventing them from growing faster than large firms.

In an effort to resolve the issue of whether costs are constant or continually declining, Hymer and Pashigian focus attention upon the dispersion of firms' growth rates around the average growth rate of any size class. Their empirical evidence[6] indicates that there is smaller variability in the growth rates of large firms than small. That is, although average growth rates of different-sized firms are equal, the dispersion of the growth rates of firms in any size class about the average growth rate in that size class declines with increasing size of firm. Again, the question is whether this evidence is more consistent with constant costs above a minimum scale of output, or continually declining costs as scale of output increases.

If costs were constant at all output levels, there would be no reason to expect the variability of growth rates of different-sized firms to differ. This conclusion remains valid even if diversification reduces the variability of profits (and hence growth rates), because small firms could diversify as much as large firms without experiencing higher unit costs. Therefore, the evidence concerning dispersion of growth rates certainly seems inconsistent with constant costs at all levels of output. It is

---

[5] Formulated originally in S. Hymer and P. Pashigian, reference (5).

[6] See also A. Singh and G. Whittington, reference (10), for similar conclusions.

not, however, inconsistent with the existence of constant costs above a minimal scale of output, for the following reasons. If economies of scale exist at low levels of output, small firms would not be able to diversify as much as large firms without experiencing higher unit costs in individual product markets. If diversification reduces the variability of profit and growth rates, the existence of economies of scale up to some minimum level of output, resulting in lower degrees of diversification by small firms than large, will result in declining variability in growth rates of larger firms, even though costs are constant above the minimum level.

Declining dispersion of growth rates as size of firm increases is compatible with the existence of constant unit costs above some minimum scale of output and also with continually declining unit costs. Although Hymer and Pashigian argue persuasively[7] that the observed reduction in dispersion is not as rapid as one would expect if costs were constant, the issue of which hypothesis is best supported by the facts remains unresolved for the present.

In view of the difficulties associated with estimating cost conditions, it is hardly surprising that empirical evidence has not yet produced general agreement regarding the shape of the LRAC curve existing in industries in practice. No matter which method of estimation is employed, however, statistical evidence seems inconsistent with the existence of diseconomies of scale in most industries within the range of firm sizes encountered to date. Similarly, all the enumerated methods of estimation indicate that economies of scale exist in many, if not most, industries. Disagreement centers around the question of whether economies of scale are exhausted beyond a certain scale of output, resulting in an L shaped long-run average cost curve, or whether they continue indefinitely. The evidence based upon statistical cost, technological study, and survival technique methods of estimation generally support the first view; evidence based upon the growth rate approach is inconclusive and can be interpreted as supporting either the first or the second view. In any event, the U shaped LRAC curve traditionally presented in economics textbooks does not seem to be encountered in practice.

RECOMMENDED READINGS

1. Alchian, A. A., "Costs and Outputs," in M. Abramovitz (ed.), *The Allocation of Economic Resources* (Palo Alto, Calif.: Stanford University Press, 1959). Reprinted in W. Breit and H. M. Hochman (eds.),

---

[7] See reference (5).

Readings in Microeconomics (New York: Holt, Rinehart and Winston, Inc., 1968).

2. Bain, J. S., "Economies of Scale, Concentration, and the Conditions of Entry in Twenty Manufacturing Industries," *American Economic Review*, 1954. Reprinted in R. B. Heflebower and G. J. Stocking (eds.) *Readings in Industrial Organization and Public Policy* (Homewood, Ill.: Richard D. Irwin, Inc., 1958); published under the sponsorship of the American Economic Association.

3. Haldi, J., and D. Whitcomb, "Economies of Scale in Industrial Plants," *Journal of Political Economy*, August 1967.

4. Hart, P. E., "The Size and Growth of Firms," *Economica*, February 1962.

5. Hymer, S., and P. Pashigian, "Firm Size and Rate of Growth," *Journal of Political Economy*, December 1962.

6. Johnston, J., *Statistical Cost Analysis* (New York: McGraw-Hill, Inc., 1960).

7. Saving, T. R., "Estimation of Optimum Size of Plant by the Survivor Technique," *Quarterly Journal of Economics*, November 1961.

8. Schwartzman, D., "Uncertainty and the Size of the Firm," *Economica*, August 1963.

9. Shepherd, W. G., "What Does the Survivor Technique Show About Economies of Scale?" *Southern Economic Journal*, July 1967.

10. Singh, A., and G. Whittington, University of Cambridge Department of Applied Economics Occasional Paper 7, *Growth, Profitability and Valuation: A Study of United Kingdom Quoted Companies* (Cambridge: Cambridge University Press, 1968).

11. Stigler, G. J., "The Economies of Scale," *Journal of Law and Economics*, Vol. 1, 1958.

12. Weiss, L. W., "The Survival Technique and the Extent of Suboptimal Capacity," *Journal of Political Economy*, June 1964.

13. Williamson, O. E., "Hierarchical Control and Optimum Firm Size," *Journal of Political Economy*, April 1967.

CHAPTER FOUR

PRICING BEHAVIOR

Although product-pricing behavior is not, itself, a feature of industrial structure, it is relevant to a study of the determinants of industrial structure since choice of price helps to determine the level of the firm's output. The first section of this chapter summarizes the main elements of coventional price theory while the second stresses the analytical irrelevance of the number of firms in price theory. In the third section, an attempt is made to place price theory in its proper perspective in relation to a broader theory of the behavior of the firm, and the last two sections deal with the theory of price discrimination.

Conventional Price Theory

In that branch of economic theory which concerns itself with the determination of product prices, the individual firm is assumed to be confronted by demand and cost conditions which are outside the firm's control. The price charged for the firm's product, and the level of the firm's output, are determined by these two sets of conditions, plus the firm's objective, which is usually assumed to be profit maximization. Given the firm's objective and cost conditions, the firm's pricing behavior will depend upon the demand conditions confronting the firm. These are depicted diagrammatically by a demand curve which shows the quantity of output the firm expects to sell at different alternative prices. It must be emphasized that the relevant demand curve reflects the expectations of the producer. The nature of such a curve depends upon the type of market in which the firm sells. Selling markets are usually classified into four different types. The market types are pure competition, monopoly, monopolistic competition, and oligopoly.

Pure competition is a market situation in which a large number of firms sell an identical product, and in which no firm is large enough to influence the market price by its output decision. Monopoly exists when there is a single seller of a product that has no close substitutes. Monopolistic competition is a market situation in which there are many firms selling differentiated varieties of a particular product, that is, the products of individual firms are not perfect substitutes for each other, and in which the actions of a single firm will have no appreciable effect on other firms. An oligopolistic market situation is one in which the number of producers is small enough for the policy decision of a single seller to affect the other firms noticeably, and in which each firm considers how its rivals will react to its own policies. The products of different firms in an oligopolistic industry can be either identical or differentiated.

The essential difference between these four market situations lies in the nature of the demand conditions confronting the individual firm, and can be briefly summarized as follows. In the purely competitive market situation, the individual firm assumes that the market price will be unaffected by its output decision—the firm's demand curve is horizontal at the prevailing market price. In the case of monopoly, the firm's demand curve is the market demand curve, that is, the demand curve facing the seller is the aggregate demand curve for that good and slopes down from left to right. In the model of monopolistic competition, each firm is confronted by a downward-sloping demand curve. The demand curve is sloped down because of product differentiation and the attachment of some consumers to particular varieties of the general class of product, which permits an individual seller to raise price relative to competitors' prices without losing all of his customers and to lower price relative to competitors' prices without attracting all or most of their customers. Furthermore, the demand curve reflects the firm's assumption that other firms will not notice, and therefore will not react to its own policy decisions by changing their prices. In contrast to monopoly, however, there are a large number of firms producing close substitutes for any individual firm's product. If each firm finds it profitable, on the basis of assuming that other firms will not change their strategies in response to its own decision to lower the price of its product, this will be true of all firms in the group. As a result, the demand curve indicating quantities which the firm will *actually* sell at different alternative prices will have a steeper slope at the existing price than the anticipated demand curve. There are, in other words, two distinct demand curves for each firm in monopolistic competition. One of these curves, labeled *dd* in Figure 4-1 (c) shows the quantities the firm expects to sell at various alternative prices if all other firms in the group hold their prices constant. This is the demand curve used by the firm in making its price and output decision, because each firm believes that other firms will not change their prices in response to its own actions. The other demand curve, labeled *DD* in Figure 4-1(c), shows the quantities which the firm will actually sell if all firms in the group change their prices simultaneously. Curve *dd* is sometimes referred to as an "other-prices-constant" demand curve, and *DD* as an "other-prices-changing" demand curve. Figure 4-1 depicts the demand conditions confronting a firm in pure competition, monopoly, and monopolistic competition.

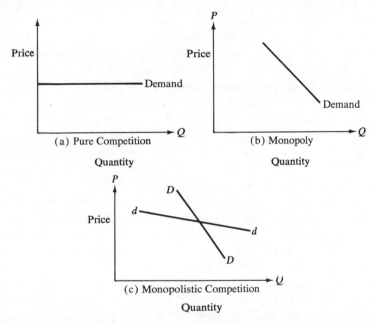

Figure 4-1   Demand Conditions in Alternative Market Situations

In the case of oligopolistic market situations, the demand conditions confronting the individual firm depend upon the firm's assumptions regarding the way in which other firms will react to its own policies, and there are numerous alternative possibilities. There is, therefore, no demand curve diagram which is typical of oligopoly.

Price theory compares and contrasts the price-cost and price-output relationships that result in each market situation. Monopolization of a purely competitive industry, for example, results in a higher price and lower level of industry output, assuming that cost and total market demand conditions do not change. There is no single equilibrium industry price-quantity combination in monopolistic competition. Since the products of individual firms are not perfect substitutes for each other, there may be more than one price involved in a group equilibrium situation.

That is, different equilibrium prices may exist for different varieties of the same class of goods. Despite this, it is possible to compare the price-output combinations of individual firms in such a market situation with the behavior of a "monopolist." Indeed, it is necessary to show that there is a difference (apart from the presence or absence of entry barriers, to be mentioned later) between the behavior of an individual firm in monopolistic competition, and a monopolist, in order to justify separate classification. The difference between the individual firm in monopolistic competition and monopoly (apart from a difference in entry conditions) can be illustrated by considering the short-run equilibrium price-quantity situation of the individual firm in these two types of market structure. In both cases, the firm assumes that its actions will not lead to reactions by other firms. In the case of monopoly, this assumption is justified, for the product has by definition no close substitutes. Any adjustments by firms in *cther* markets do not affect the market demand curve. In contrast, in monopolistic competition, although each firm expects its actions to go unnoticed because of the large number of competitors, other firms do not behave as each individual firm anticipates. The actual demand curve confronting the firm in monopolistic competition is steeper in slope than the demand curve used by the firm in arriving at its price-output decision. In equilibrium, the optimal price-quantity combination selected by the monopolistic competitor will equate the marginal cost of production with the marginal revenue associated with the subjective demand curve showing the quantities the firm expects to sell at different prices if other firms' behavior remains unchanged. Since the actual demand curve, showing quantities the firm could sell at different prices if other firms pursue similar policies, is steeper than the subjective demand curve at the selected optimal price-quantity combination, actual marginal revenue must be less than the subjective marginal revenue at that quantity of output. Each individual firm in the group could increase its own profits, and therefore total industry profits, by producing a smaller level of output of each variety of the product.

Oligopolistic market situations are many and varied. As already explained, the common characteristic of these models is that a firm makes some explicit assumptions about the reactions of other firms to its own strategies. The firm's pricing behavior will depend upon the precise nature of these assumptions, and the resulting equilibrium industry price, or set of prices if the products of individual firms are differentiated, can range from a purely competitive price to a monopoly price.

The different market situations of conventional price theory are contrasted with respect to the different price-marginal cost relationships that result in each case. We shall return to analyze the significance of such relationships for resource allocation in Chapter 10. Apart from the price-marginal cost relationship, a further distinction is usually made between the different market situations according to the conditions of entry existing in each case. In pure competition and monopolistic competition, entry is assumed to be easy. In monopoly and oligopoly, entry is assumed to be barred. Conditions of entry affect the relationship between the equilibrium price and average cost of products marketed. The significance of entry barriers is analyzed in greater detail in Chapter 7.

Importance of Assumed Reactions Rather Than Numbers

The different equilibrium price-marginal cost relationships associated with the market types of conventional price theory do not depend upon differences between the number of firms in each market situation. They depend instead upon the belief about the policy of its rivals attributed to the individual firm in each market situation.

Given the number of firms in a market, a different pattern of behavior will result depending upon the assumption made by an individual firm concerning the reaction of other firms in that group to its own strategies. Conversely, given the belief about the policy of its rivals, the behavior of the firm will be the same whether its rivals are one or many.

These propositions can be illustrated by considering an industry consisting of two firms producing an identical product. If each firm is assumed to believe that its competitor will maintain its output constant (and, implicitly, match price) irrespective of the price charged by the firm, the equilibrium price-cost relationship will be identical to that reached in a monopolistically competitive market situation. Figure 4–2 depicts such an equilibrium. Each firm equates the marginal cost of producing its product with the marginal revenue (MR_c) expected to accrue to the firm if its rival produces an unchanged level of output at different alternative prices that could be charged by the first firm.

Provided that each individual firm continues to assume that its competitors will maintain their output constant in response to its own strategies, increases in the number of firms in the group shifts the demand curve facing an individual firm bodily to the left without altering the slope; it does not make the demand curve facing the individual firm horizontal and thus it does not result in a purely competitive solution in which equilibrium price equals marginal cost. At any price, the elasticity of demand for the product of an individual firm will be increased, because price elasticity of demand is defined as the product of the inverse of the slope of the demand curve and the ratio of price to

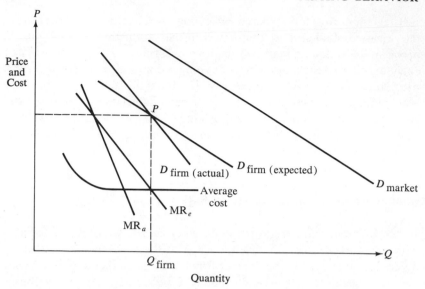

Figure 4–2   Industry Equilibrium with Two Firms Assuming Rivals'
Output Constant

quantity, and although the slope is not changed, the quantity demanded
at any price will be less. However, because the demand curve slopes
down, average revenue exceeds marginal revenue, and the profit-maximizing price remains above marginal revenue and therefore above
marginal cost no matter how many firms are in the industry.

To obtain the horizontal demand curve of pure competition it is
necessary to change the firm's assumption about the policy of its rivals;
what is required, instead of the assumption that rivals keep output
constant, is the explicit assumption that each individual firm believes
that changes in its output do not alter price. If, for example, firms assume
that their competitors will not change price in response to their individual actions, the individual firm's demand curve at a price slightly
below that of its rivals will be horizontal, up to the total quantity demanded by the market at that price. Attempts to undercut rivals' prices
will result in a situation in which the equilibrium industry price will
equal marginal cost of production in individual firms irrespective of the
number of firms in the industry—with two firms as well as with a large
number.

These remarks emphasize that the distinction between pure competition and monopolistic competition depends not on numbers, but on
the beliefs attributed to the firms involved in each situation. Also, the
first example demonstrates that product differentiation is not necessarily
required in order to yield an equilibrium price-cost relationship identical
to that achieved in monopolistic competition.

Finally, it can be demonstrated that if each firm assumes that other firms in the industry will imitate both its price and output strategy, the equilibrium industry price and output combination will (assuming constant marginal costs identical for each firm, and a linear total market demand curve) be the same as that resulting under conditions of monopoly, irrespective of the number of firms in the group. This case is treated in more detail in Chapter 7.

It is possible to introduce additional elements into the analysis in order to establish a link between pricing behavior and the number of firms in an industry. For example, the reaction of a particular firm's rivals depends upon whether the firms are aware of its moves. Information regarding one firm's actions may be transmitted to other firms by the resulting variations in the sales of those firms. Other things being equal, it may seem reasonable to expect that the absolute disturbance experienced by an individual firm as the result of another firm's actions will be smaller, the larger the number of firms operating in the industry. If the ease of detecting rivals' actions decreases with increases in the number of rivals, numbers may affect the anticipated reactions, and therefore behavior, of individual firms in a particular industry.

Although there are persuasive a priori reasons why the number of firms in an industry might influence the nature of an individual firm's assumptions regarding the reactions of other firms to its policies, and therefore the firm's behavior, these hypotheses must be tested with respect to the facts in any particular situation. These matters are treated further in Chapter 6.

Partial Equilibrium versus General Equilibrium Analysis of the Behavior of the Firm

Conventional price theory focuses attention upon the determination of the price and level of output of a firm's product. The individual firm is assumed to be confronted by demand and cost conditions which are outside the firm's control; these conditions, plus the firm's objective, determine the price charged by the firm, and the level of its output. The essence of much business behavior, however, is a conscious attempt to influence demand and cost conditions by spending money on activities, such as advertising and research and development, which shape preferences, add to the body of knowledge, and adopt new knowledge, in order to protect and expand market positions. If a firm can influence the demand and cost conditions for its product by varying the levels of its advertising, R&D, or other outlays, it is necessary to regard the conventional treatment of a firm's pricing behavior as a partial equilibrium analysis of the firm's behavior, in contrast to a general equilibrium analysis. In a general equilibrium approach to the behavior of a firm, the process by which the optimal levels of all the firm's policy variables are simultaneously determined is investigated; in a partial equilibrium analysis, attention is focused upon the determination of fewer policy variables by assuming that some of the firm's policy variables are at their respective optimal levels.

In conventional price theory it is assumed that all policy variables which influence the firm's demand and cost conditions, such as levels of advertising and R&D outlays, have already been determined, and the analysis focuses attention upon the determination of the remaining policy variables, namely price and level of the firm's output. The profits associated with a particular price depend, however, upon the level of the firm's investment in activities, including advertising and R&D, which influence the demand and cost conditions associated with the firm's product. The profitability of a particular level of investment in these activities depends, in turn, upon the price charged for the resulting product. Levels of investment in activities which influence demand and cost conditions, and the price of the firm's product, may be simultaneously determined by the firm's decision makers. One cannot then show the determination of one of these policy variables in isolation, except in the artificial context of a partial equilibrium analysis. In Chapter 5, a general equilibrium approach to the determination of price, output, and advertising outlays is illustrated diagrammatically.

Most aspects of a firm's behavior are closely related. To a large extent this is attributable to the fact that the funds available to a firm, in the form of depreciation allowances, profits, and additional external finance, are limited at any particular point in time. The firm's decision concerning the level of its investment in current production activities, in advertising activities, and in R&D or other activities may be made by weighing the effects of spending its investment funds on one activity rather than another, and by comparing the anticipated contribution of each activity to the decision-makers' objectives. The firm's decision makers will achieve a balance in the distribution of the firm's limited investment funds between these different activities which best accomplishes the decision-makers' objectives in the light of their own evaluation of how the different activities contribute towards these objectives.[1]

The inherent simultaneity of many of the firm's decisions necessitates a general equilibrium approach to the behavior of the firm, rather than a partial equilibrium approach. A complete understanding of the re-

---

[1] See D. Mueller, "The Firm's Decision Process: An Econometric Investigation," *Quarterly Journal of Economics*, February, 1967, for empirical evidence indicating the simultaneity of many of a firm's decisions.

lationship between different aspects of a firm's behavior is essential in order to assist formulation of logically consistent public policy measures designed to influence business conduct. A policy which is designed to influence one aspect of the firm's behavior will very likely, as a result of this simultaneity, also influence other aspects of the firm's behavior. Public policy measures imposed without regard to the effect of the measures on all aspects of the firm's behavior may have side effects which, on balance, render the measures undesirable. For example, the profitability of R&D investment depends upon anticipated prices received for the resulting products. These prices depend, in part, upon the anticipated extent of price competition in the markets concerned. A policy designed to increase price competition in a particular industry might, in addition, reduce R&D investment and result in an undesirable reduction in the rate of new product introduction.

Uniform Pricing and Price Discrimination

Before we leave the subject of pricing behavior, a summary of the theory of price discrimination is appropriate. We shall have occasion to refer to this in several later chapters. Price discrimination can be defined as the practice of selling the same kind of product or service at different prices to different purchasers. For simplicity, the following analysis assumes that the market for a particular product is separated into two markets.

Separation of the total market for a particular product into a number of independent markets is essential before price discrimination is *possible*; whether it is *profitable* to charge different prices even when this is possible is a separate question. In diagrammatic terms, separation of markets means that each of the demand curves D_1 and D_2 in Figure 4–3, representing respectively the demand conditions in the two markets, is independent of the price charged in the other market.

In order to maximize profits, a firm should observe the following two rules in deciding on the level of its output and the allocation of that output among the different markets.

Rule one is that any given level of output produced should be allocated between the different markets in such a manner as to equate the marginal revenue in each market. If marginal revenue differs between markets, it follows that a reallocation of the total output currently being sold in these markets is possible; this will increase total revenue and therefore, because the total cost of that level of output will be unchanged, also profits. Rule two is that the firm should produce a total level of output which equates marginal revenue, which will be the same

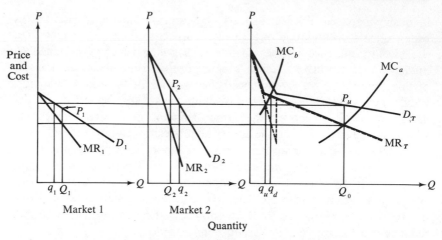

Figure 4–3 A Price Discrimination Model

in all markets if rule one is observed, to the marginal cost of producing the product.

Diagrammatically, horizontal summation of MR_1 and MR_2, the marginal revenue curves in each market, yields a curve, MR_T, which shows the total marginal revenue associated with a given level of total output when the allocation of output between the markets satisfies rule one. The profit-maximizing level of total output is that output level which equates this total marginal revenue curve with the marginal cost of producing the product. If MC_a represents the marginal cost of producing the product, Q_0 is the profit-maximizing level of output. The optimal allocation of this total output level between the two markets, and therefore the price to be charged in each market, follows automatically from observing rule one. Diagrammatically, the optimal allocation is obtained by extending a horizontal line at the level where MR_T intersects MC_a, until it intersects the marginal revenue curve in each individual market. Thus, in Figure 4–3, Q_1 and Q_2 are the profit-maximizing quantities in market 1 and market 2 respectively, while P_1 and P_2 are the respective prices charged.

In Figure 4–3, maximum profits are earned by charging a different price in each market. Price will be higher in the market with a more price-inelastic demand at the optimal quantity associated with that market. This can be demonstrated by referring to the following relationship between price, marginal revenue, and price elasticity of demand:

$$\text{marginal revenue} = \text{price}\left(1 - \frac{1}{\text{price elasticity of demand}}\right)$$

The relationship is valid for the level of output sold in each separate market.[2] Because marginal revenue associated with the optimal level of output sold in each market is equal, the ratio of price to marginal revenue will be higher in the market in which the price elasticity of demand is smallest at the optimal quantity. The last phrase must be added in view of the fact that price elasticity of demand may vary along any given demand curve and demand curves cannot be said to be more or less elastic without reference to a specific point on the demand curve.

It is useful to consider the effect of prohibiting price discrimination on the level of output and prices in each market. If price discrimination is not possible, the individual *demand curves* in each market, and not the marginal revenue curves as in the previous example, are summed horizontally to yield D_T, a demand curve showing the total quantity of the firm's product demanded at any price which is uniform in all markets. The marginal revenue curve associated with D_T shows the marginal revenue associated with any level of output if prices are uniform in all markets. This marginal revenue curve, shown by the dotted line in Figure 4–3, is discontinuous, in contrast to the continuous marginal revenue curve confronting the firm if it is permitted to discriminate.

If cost conditions are represented by MC_a in the diagram, the optimal level of the firm's total output remains unchanged if price discrimination is prohibited. The allocation of this output between markets will change, however, and the firm's profits will therefore be reduced. The firm's profits must be reduced because formerly, with discrimination, marginal revenue is equal in all markets; a change in the allocation of output between markets must therefore leave marginal revenue in each market unequal, which implies that total revenue is reduced. At a uniform price, P_u, in all markets, the allocation of Q_0 between markets is q_1 and q_2 respectively.

In other circumstances, the total level of the firms output may either

---

[2] Total revenue in any market is equal to the quantity sold in that market, Q, multiplied by the selling price, P. That is,

$$\text{TR} = PQ$$

Marginal revenue $= \dfrac{d(\text{TR})}{dQ} = P + Q\,\dfrac{dP}{dQ} = P\left(1 + \dfrac{Q}{P}\,\dfrac{dP}{dQ}\right)$

Price-elasticity of demand is defined as $-\dfrac{dQ}{dP}\,\dfrac{P}{Q}$

Therefore, marginal revenue $=$ price $\left(1 - \dfrac{1}{\text{price elasticity of demand}}\right)$

increase or decrease if price discrimination is prohibited. For example, if marginal cost conditions were depicted by the line MC_b in the above diagram, total output will be greater with price discrimination $(= q_d)$ than without $(= q_u)$. As explained in Chapter 10, some arguments against permitting price discrimination revolve around the price differences themselves, rather than around output differences. However, as the preceding analysis demonstrates, the two considerations cannot always be disentangled.

Before we leave the subject of price discrimination, it is necessary to elaborate upon the definition given at the beginning of this section, particularly the concept of "the same kind of product or service." Price discrimination may be defined more precisely as the practice of selling products at prices disproportionate to the marginal costs of the products sold. The products need not be identical; differentiation may be a means of separating the total market of a particular seller and is the essence of some types of price discrimination. It follows from the above definition that differential pricing need not be discriminatory. Thus, for example, a seller who sells a physically identical product to buyers located at different distances from the seller will not be discriminating if he charges delivered prices which reflect the difference in transportation cost between seller and each buyer. Conversely, price discrimination may occur even in the absence of a price differential. This will be the case, for example, if two buyers of the same kind of product are charged identical prices by a single seller, but the seller incurs different production, selling, or transportation costs in serving them. In order to discover whether price discrimination exists, it is necessary to have information concerning not only the prices charged, but also the costs incurred by the seller.

The points dealt with in the preceding paragraph have important implications for public policy measures relating to the practice of price discrimination, yet are sometimes ignored. In the United States, for example, Section 2a of the Robinson-Patman Act makes price discrimination illegal if it tends to lessen competition substantially. However, a prerequisite for finding an illegal price discrimination under Section 2a is a *price difference* resulting from sales by an individual seller of the same kind of goods at a lower price to one purchaser than to another. Unless a price differential between two customers is established, the courts will not consider the further legal issue of whether the price discrimination may injure competitors, or tend to lessen competition substantially, or tend to create a monopoly. Hence, the law will omit cases of price discrimination which occur whenever products with different marginal costs are sold at the same price.

Delivered Pricing versus Mill Pricing

A firm may be able to control the degree of separation of the total market for its product. In such a situation, the decision of whether to discriminate on a price basis will involve comparing the additional profitability of price discrimination, compared to uniform pricing, with the costs of separating the market.

A relatively costless method of separating the market, available notably to firms producing a product with high transportation costs, consists of choosing to quote a delivered price rather than a factory, or mill, price. Under a delivered price system, the purchaser is quoted a price which covers transportation, and the seller assumes responsibility for transporting the product to the buyer. In contrast, under a mill price system the seller quotes a price which does not cover the cost of transporting the product from seller to buyer, and the buyer is left to arrange transportation.

The manner in which choice of a delivered price system, as opposed to a mill price system, can separate the total market of a seller, and permit the firm to discriminate between different geographical sectors of its market, can be illustrated by the following example. Consider a firm selling to two groups of consumers located in two different geographical areas A and B. For simplicity, assume that transportation costs between seller and each group of consumers are the same. Assume further, that conditions of demand for the product differ in each area and that elasticity of demand for the product at any particular price is less in area A than in area B. This means that if the firm were to charge the same price in both markets, the marginal revenue associated with the quantity sold in market B would be higher than the marginal revenue associated with the quantity sold in market A. That is, the firm could earn more profits by charging a higher price in A and a lower price in B, thereby causing a reallocation of output from A to B without changing the level of its total output. If the firm attempts to charge a different mill price to purchasers in the different areas, discrimination tends to be thwarted by resale from low-price to high-price consumers. Apart from the problem of attempting to prevent low-price purchases from being resold to the high-price area, discrimination will be difficult to implement because buyers will not willingly disclose their locations. A necessary condition for the practice of geographical price discrimination is knowledge of the location of prospective customers. Without this information the seller who wishes to discriminate does not know which of the two mill prices to quote to them. Consumers in the high mill-price area will not willingly disclose this fact, hoping thereby to get the lower mill-price quotation. The firm wishing to discriminate will be faced by the prospect of having to check customers' locations.

Delivered pricing reduces the profitability of resale because buyers at the low "mill net return" (delivered price minus transportation cost) must take delivery in the low mill-price area. The mill net return received by the seller per unit sold in each market can differ by an amount equal to the cost of transporting the product between the two geographical areas before resale from low-price to high-price area becomes profitable. Also, since all prices are delivered prices, customers are forced to disclose their locations in order to obtain quotations.

Charging a delivered price need not mean that the seller actually performs the transportation itself; the seller may simply hire the services of some independent transportation firm. If the firm actually performs the transportation itself, the situation is a special case of separating the market by (forward) vertical integration, which is discussed in Chapter 8.

RECOMMENDED READINGS

1. Archibald, G. C., " 'Large' and 'Small' Numbers in the Theory of the Firm," *Manchester School,* 1959.
2. Leftwich, R. H., *The Price System and Resource Allocation,* 3d ed. (New York: Holt, Rinehart and Winston, Inc., 1966), Chapter 6.
3. Machlup, F., "Characteristics and Types of Price Discrimination," in G. J. Stigler (ed.) *Business Concentration and Price Policy* (Princeton, N.J.: Princeton University Press, 1955).
4. ————, "Monopoly and Competition: A Classification of Market Positions," *American Economic Review,* September 1937.
5. Olson, M., and D. McFarland, "The Restoration of Pure Monopoly and the Concept of the Industry," *Quarterly Journal of Economics,* November 1962.
6. Robinson, Joan, *The Economics of Imperfect Competition* (London: Macmillan & Co., Ltd., 1933), Chapters 15 and 16.
7. Stigler, G. J., "A Theory of Oligopoly," *Journal of Political Economy,* February 1964.

CHAPTER FIVE

PRODUCT DIFFERENTIATION

Product differentiation exists if the products of different firms in the same industry are not perfect substitutes for each other from the point of view of buyers of the industry's product(s).

From the point of view of an individual firm, efforts to differentiate its product from those of other firms are motivated by the same consideration that prompts the firm to invest in productive activities, namely, the pursuit of particular objectives, such as profit maximization. Product differentiation activities are aimed at influencing the demand conditions for the firm's product.

The methods used by firms to attempt to differentiate their products in consumers' minds are many and varied. Generally, however, product differentiation is based either upon advertising or differences in the physical characteristics of the firms' product(s). Advertising activities, style changes, and research and development activities are the major strategies available to a firm for differentiating its product.

Advertising

Advertising is a strategy for influencing the shape or position of the demand curve for a firm's product without changing the physical characteristics of the product.

As was pointed out in the preceding chapter in the section entitled Partial Equilibrium versus General Equilibrium Analysis of the Behavior of the Firm, the optimal level of a firm's investment in advertising, and optimal price (or what amounts to the same thing, the optimal

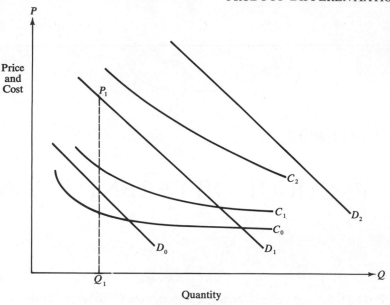

Figure 5–1   Simultaneous Determination of Price, Output,
and Advertising Levels

level of investment in current production activities) may be simultaneously determined. Figure 5–1 illustrates this process diagrammatically. The demand curve labeled D_0 indicates the number of units of output the firm expects to sell at various alternative prices if it did not advertise. The average cost curve labeled C_0 indicates the average cost of production at different levels of output. If the firm can influence its demand curve by advertising, associated with each level of advertising there will be a different demand curve representing the demand conditions anticipated at that level of advertising outlay. For example, D_1 represents the demand conditions anticipated at a level of advertising outlays A_1; D_2 represents the demand conditions anticipated at a higher level of advertising A_2, and so on. Similarly, associated with each level of advertising there will be a different average total cost curve indicating the average cost of producing and distributing different levels of output of the firm's product. At a level of advertising A_1, for example, the firm's average total cost curve is C_1; it is obtained by adding a rectangular hyperbola representing the fixed level of advertising outlays A_1 vertically to C_0. The advertising outlays necessary to secure any given state of demand enter the firm's cost function as a fixed cost, that is, a cost which does not vary with the quantity of output. Therefore, the curve of average advertising costs will be a rectangular hyperbola, that is, average advertising cost multiplied by quantity of output is a constant.

In order to, say, maximize profits, the firm must compare the maximum profit (total revenue minus production and advertising cost) associated with each pair of demand and cost curves. This will involve selecting a price-output combination which maximizes profits from each pair of demand and cost curves. With an advertising level A_1, for example, the profit-maximizing price is P_1, at which the quantity sold is Q_1. Profits will be maximized by choosing a pair of demand and cost curves (that is, a level of advertising) and a price, which yield the maximum profits, subject to the constraint that the level of investment in production and advertising activities which are implied by this combination is no greater than the firm's available investment funds. The profits associated with any price depend upon the level of advertising and consequent position of the demand (and cost) curves; the profits associated with any given level of advertising depend upon the price charged at that level of advertising. The optimal level of advertising and optimal price (that is, optimal level of investment in current production activities) will be simultaneously determined.

The distinction between general and partial equilibrium analysis, referred to in the previous chapter, can also be illustrated using this example. If A_i is the optimal level of advertising outlays, one can assume that this is determined (hence the demand and cost conditions will be determined), and focus attention on the "determination" of price using one demand curve and one cost curve. Likewise, if P_i is the optimal price, one can take this as given, and focus attention upon the "determination" of the optimal level of advertising outlay as shown in Figure 5–2.

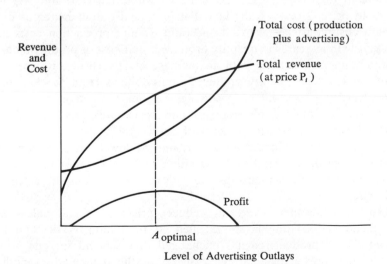

Figure 5–2   Partial Equilibrium Determination of Advertising Outlays

Neither of these approaches, however, shows the way in which price and level of advertising are selected by the firm's decision makers, if price and advertising level are simultaneously determined by comparison of all price-advertising outlay combinations.

The previous example assumed that the firm was free to choose the price of its product. A similar analysis applies, however, if the price which a firm can charge is predetermined by conventional, oligopolistic, legal, or other considerations. The only difference that this makes to the previous example is that the firm must compare the profits associated with each pair of demand and cost curves when the price charged is the same in all circumstances. It still remains true that the optimal level of the firm's output, and optimal level of advertising outlays, are simultaneously determined.

Advertising, Unit Costs, and Price

The above diagrammatic analysis can be employed to explain the logic of the argument that advertising reduces price.. This is, of course, by implication, the other side of the argument that abolishing advertising outlays will raise price. Since advertising increases the total cost of producing and distributing a particular product, total revenue must be higher to cover advertising outlays than it would have to be in their absence. However, average revenue (price) per unit of output sold need not increase in order to satisfy this condition. Total revenue is price multiplied by quantity sold, and if quantity sold increases, an increase in total revenue can be achieved without necessitating an increase in price. However, the fact that increased output increases production costs must be taken into account. If unit production costs are constant with increases in quantity produced, unit cost of production and distribution *must* increase with an increase in advertising, irrespective of the increase in quantity produced. This follows from the fact that unit advertising cost will be positive no matter how large the output. Therefore, to obtain a reduction in unit costs, unit production costs must *fall* with increases in the level of output.

It follows that, in order for advertising to lower price, advertising must increase the quantity sold *and* either unit profits must be reduced or unit production costs must decline with increases in output, as shown in Figure 5–3.

The argument that advertising reduces prices is invalid unless the aforementioned conditions are satisfied. If total industry demand for the advertised product remains unchanged, the demand for one firm's product can only expand at the expense of the demand for another

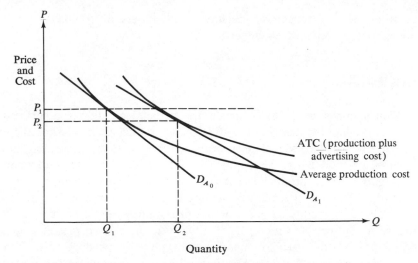

Figure 5–3   Necessary Conditions for Advertising to Reduce Price

firm's product. Any tendency for unit production costs to decline in one firm will be offset by the reverse tendency in firms experiencing a reduction in demand. In these circumstances, advertising can only lower industry price if some firms are driven out of the industry, enabling the surviving firms to reap economies of scale in production. If total industry demand for the advertised product increases as a result of advertising, it is possible for all existing firms to experience increases in demand for their individual products, permitting economies of scale in production to be reaped, and industry price to be lowered.

If one firm in a particular industry increases its advertising outlays, and other firms retaliate sufficiently to return the demand conditions confronting individual firms to the original state, advertising must simply raise the price of the product in question. In these circumstances, no single firm can afford to reduce its advertising efforts unilaterally, for it will thereby lose its share of the market. Although a reduction of advertising by all firms will simply reduce costs and increase industry profits at the existing industry price, firms may be unable to agree to this among themselves.

It should be emphasized that the presence of an increase in demand plus scale economies does not guarantee that advertising will lower price, merely that lower price is possible. The profit-maximizing price with advertising may be the same, higher, or lower, than the profit-maximizing price in the absence of advertising.

Finally, as will be explained in Chapter 10, the effect of advertising on price does not determine whether advertising is beneficial from the point of view of consumers, including purchasers of products whose prices may be reduced by advertising.

Style Changes

A firm may attempt to influence the demand conditions associated with its product by changing the style of its product. It is possible for a firm to change the style of its product without actually increasing the level of its total costs. Thus, for example, a certain total outlay on packaging a firm's product is compatible with frequent changes in the style of packaging. Alternatively, it may be possible for style changes to be achieved by modifying items of the firm's capital equipment when it wears out and needs to be replaced. However, there is no reason why a firm should restrict itself to changing the style of its product *only* when physical obsolescence permits this without increasing costs. Style changes require inputs, which cost money. The input cost associated with a particular *rate* of change of style will, however, be a fixed cost independent of the level of output produced by the firm between style changes.

The influence of style changes on the structure of the United States automobile industry may be mentioned by way of illustration. It has been argued[1] that the use of style changes as a market weapon may have been responsible for the demise of all save the largest firms in the industry. The argument, in brief, is as follows. The dies used in automobile manufacture, which are an insert in a large metal stamping press, relate to a particular style of automobile. These dies are indivisable in the sense that the minimal durability requirements to punch even one panel result automatically in a prolonged physical life for any given die. Firms producing larger rates of output per period will use up their dies more quickly than firms producing lower rates of output. If larger firms replace their dies with dies embodying a new style, and if smaller firms follow suit and change the style of their product with the same frequency, the die cost per automobile produced will be higher for firms producing smaller rates of output. Associated with a single style change, there is a minimum cost, the cost of a new die, and the greater the number of units of output over which the cost of the die is spread, the lower the die cost per automobile produced. Given industry price, accelerated style changes involving higher style change costs per period will, it has been argued, drive small firms from the industry.

---

[1] See J. A. Menge, "Style Change Costs as a Market Weapon," *Quarterly Journal of Economics,* November 1962. Reference (7).

The validity of this argument rests upon a number of crucial assumptions. The basic requirement is that style change costs are independent of the level of a firm's output, resulting in economies of scale. Another assumption is that smaller firms follow suit and change style with the same frequency as firms producing larger rates of output per period, and that there exists a fixed industry price which must be adhered to by all firms. In other words, the alternative competitive strategy of less frequent style changes and reduced price is ruled out for small firms.

It must be stressed that the previous argument is not peculiar to style change costs. It is merely a special case of the proposition that if there are economies of scale in an industry, whether caused by style change costs, advertising, or some other category of costs that are independent of the scale of a firm's output, small firms will be unable to survive either price competition or, given industry price, cost competition. That is, provided there is competition in the industry, whether price or cost competition, the size of firms that are able to remain and compete in an industry will be influenced by economies of scale.

Research and Development Activities

The identifying characteristic of R&D activities is that they produce new knowledge, including knowledge of how to apply existing inventions to commercial purposes. The new knowledge resulting from a firm's R&D activities may be embodied in new products, or may result in less costly methods of producing products already marketed by the firm.

A profit-maximizing firm will only undertake a research project if the total R&D cost is exceeded by the present value of the additional profits expected to accrue to the firm as a result of the R&D outlays. These profits will depend upon the anticipated effect of the R&D investment upon the demand or cost conditions confronting the firm. The relationship between different levels of R&D investment and a firm's cost and demand conditions could be exhibited diagrammatically in a similar manner to that employed in the first section of this chapter, substituting R&D expenditures for advertising expenditures. Since current R&D outlays yield results, and revenues, only after a considerable lapse of time, the curves in the diagram would have to relate to present values of future expected revenues (or cost reductions). Also, since it is in the nature of R&D investment to change the characteristics of the firm's product, the x axis would no longer refer, as is the case with advertising, to a physically unchanging product.

A notable feature of R&D inputs is that they are indivisable below a certain size, that is, there is a minimum size of R&D input, which can, however, vary between industries. One cannot hire half a research chemist or scientist, or conduct research without laboratory facilities which are, below a certain size, indivisable. A fixed minimum size of R&D input means that firms with limited access to investment funds may be unable to consider R&D as a competitive strategy, even though the firm might expect such a strategy to be potentially profitable. Empirical evidence[2] shows that within industries which engage in R&D activities, there is indeed a minimum size of firm below which firms do not engage in R&D activities. There is, of course, nothing to prevent small firms from engaging in cooperative R&D ventures that are outside the scope of each individual firm's financial resources, or from hiring the services of independent R&D organizations. Either of these alternatives would, in effect, enable small firms to share costs of minimum-sized indivisible R&D organizations. There are, however, several reasons why this approach will not be as efficient as performing the same level of R&D activities in the research department of a single firm.[3]

First, even if the firms engaging in cooperative research or utilizing the services of an independent research organization are members of the same industry, and the resulting R&D output is the same as would result if the research were carried out by the research department of a single firm, there are likely to be additional costs, which are absent in the case of a single firm, in carrying out the research. The planning, coordination, and evaluation of research by a number of independent firms is likely to require more resources than the coordination of the same amount of research undertaken by a single firm. Independent R&D organizations argue, for example, that each client needs at least one full-time trained man on its own staff in order to communicate clearly the nature of the project it wishes done, to evaluate the proposal competently, and to interpret and make effective use of the results. In one firm carrying out the same aggregate amount of research, only one such man would be needed.

Second, apart from the costs of carrying out the R&D activities provided by a minimum-sized R&D organization, the total benefits anticipated by firms sharing the cost may be smaller than in the case of a

---

[2] See, for example, reference (9), National Science Foundation, *Basic Research, Applied Research, and Development in Industry 1965,* NSF 67-12 (Washington, D.C.: U.S. Government Printing Office, 1967). Also see J. W. Markham, "Market Structure, Business Conduct and Innovation," *American Economic Review,* May 1965 (supplement) for a useful summary of empirical studies of the relationship between firm size, concentration, and R&D activities.

[3] In this connection, see W. L. Baldwin, "Contracted Research & the Case for Big Business," *Journal of Political Economy,* June 1962, reference (2).

single firm. The single firm will employ the results of the R&D activity to its best advantage, whereas a number of small firms in a particular industry are potential competitors and may, for example, expect the prices received for products resulting from R&D activities to be lower as a result of competition between themselves. For this reason, a group of small firms in the same industry may be less likely to engage in R&D than a single large firm.

Third, if the firms engaging in cooperative research or employing independent R&D organizations are members of different industries, the R&D output resulting from the use of minimum-sized R&D inputs may be lower than results if the same amount of R&D input specializes in solving the problems of one industry. That is, there may be increasing returns to scale in the performance of R&D activities in particular industries. A research chemist, or scientist, who spends equal parts of his time working for two firms in different industries may produce for each industry an amount of new knowledge that is less than half the amount which would be obtained if he devoted all his time to the problem of one industry. In these circumstances, the services of independent research organizations may not be considered an effective substitute by firms unable to bear the whole cost of indivisible R&D facilities alone; such firms may prefer alternative strategies, such as advertising coupled with rapid imitation of new developments to counter the moves of large firms in the same industry possessing their own internal research facilities.

Product Differentiation Activity Mix

Advertising, style changes, and R&D activities are alternative methods of attempting to influence the demand conditions confronting a firm. The combination of these activities chosen by any particular firm will depend upon the firm's own evaluation of how the individual activities contribute to its objectives; the firm's decision regarding the combination of methods may be made by comparing the anticipated effects of spending its investment funds on each of these strategies.[4]

The magnitude of expected returns associated with spending a given amount of investment funds on any of the alternative strategies will be influenced by a number of factors connected with the characteristics

---

[4] See reference (8), D. Mueller, "The Firm's Decision Process: An Econometric Investigation," *Quarterly Journal of Economics,* February 1967, for empirical evidence indicating the simultaneity of a firm's output, advertising, & R.&D. decisions.

of the market in which the firm sells. Whether a firm will consider engaging in R&D activities, for example, will be influenced by a set of conditions sometimes described under the heading of technological opportunity. In some industries, the broad advance of science and technology provides a continuous supply of exploitable new technical possibilities; in other industries, the prospect of R&D investment yielding significant new knowledge culminating in marketable products or cost-reducing processes is relatively limited. There may be little scope for differences in style in some industries; products which are the raw materials and inputs of other firms must often meet rigid specifications in terms of physical dimensions or chemical and other attributes, leaving little room for variety in style. Styling is more likely to be used as a market weapon in consumer good industries, where the product fulfills no simple technical function, but rather can satisfy many different sorts of personal needs or uses.

The anticipated return from advertising will likewise be influenced by the characteristics of buyers' information in the market in which a firm operates.[5] Advertising is one of several possible methods of providing potential buyers with knowledge of the identity of sellers, the nature of the products offered, and the terms upon which they are offered. If buyers were already completely informed of these matters, advertising would not affect their behavior and therefore would not be a strategy considered by firms. The benefits of advertising, from the point of view of a firm, will therefore depend upon the amount of information a given level of advertising outlay provides to buyers. This, in turn, will be influenced by a number of factors connected with the nature of the firm's product. The effectiveness of advertising in providing information will depend upon the extent to which potential buyers bother to search for information. The amount of search undertaken by an individual buyer will depend upon the benefits anticipated by the buyer as a result of searching for information, and upon the cost of this search. The benefits might, for example, consist of the saving in expenditure expected as a result of the search, while the cost of acquiring information is largely the opportunity cost of time spent on this activity. The anticipated benefits will tend to be greater, the larger the buyer's expenditure on the product; therefore, all other things being equal, one would expect advertising to yield greater returns in the case of products which occupy a relatively large fraction of a buyer's total expenditure. Another factor influencing the extent to which buyers search for information, and therefore the effectiveness of advertising, will be the frequency of purchase of a product by individual buyers. Given a stable

---

[5] See G. J. Stigler, "The Economics of Information," *Journal of Political Economy,* June 1961, reference (10).

and unchanging population of buyers, the amount of search per buyer will be greater the more infrequently the product is purchased, since there will be a greater need to refresh memories. Given a stable population of potential buyers in a market, and the amount of search undertaken per buyer, a given level of advertising will provide more information, and will therefore be more effective, the greater the turnover of buyers in the market. These factors influencing the effectiveness of a given amount of advertising apply even though the number of sellers in a market, the nature of their products, and the terms upon which these are offered remain unchanged. If technology, products, and terms are changing, the amount of information supplied to potential buyers by a given level of advertising will be greater, and in general, a given level of advertising will provide more information, and will be more effective, the greater the rate of change of these variables over time. There is in practice less advertising of producer goods than consumer goods. This difference may in part be accounted for by the fact that in the absence of advertising, producers are usually better informed than are consumers regarding the sellers and characteristics of the products they buy. Moreover, the turnover of buyers (and sellers) is likely to be less in the case of producer goods than consumer goods, while the frequency of purchase may be higher in the case of producer goods, resulting in a need for less information of the memory refreshing variety.

The expected returns associated with the different kinds of product differentiation strategy may differ in respect of the time lapse before they accrue. The returns from current R&D investment, for example, will probably be expected to accrue after a longer period than the return to current advertising outlays, for a long lag often occurs between the initiation of research project and the creation of something of marketable value. This does not, of course, create a general preference on the part of decision makers for advertising (or style changes) as opposed to R&D investment as a competitive strategy. However, given the rate at which a decision maker discounts the future, strategies yielding expected returns at more distant points in time must be more profitable relative to strategies yielding earlier expected returns, in order to induce the decision maker to undertake the former.

Uncertainty will also play a part in influencing the firm's choice between different product differentiation strategies. The outcome of all activities, even current production activities, is uncertain; that is, the anticipated outcome of any strategy will take the form of a probability distribution of expected outcomes, rather than a single-valued magnitude. Although the expected profitability (that is, the mathematical expectation of profit) of different strategies may be similar, a firm may choose between them on the basis of other characteristics of the proba-

bility distribution associated with each strategy. The large variance of
the profit probability distribution of an R&D project may cause a firm
to prefer a strategy with a smaller variance of possible outcomes, for
example.

The relative profitability of different types of product differentiation
activity will be influenced by the firm's expectations regarding the behavior of its rivals. The extent to which it pays a firm to imitate its
rivals' strategies is the subject of much current research and debate.
In certain circumstances, the firm's optimal strategy is to imitate its
rivals' actions. This can be demonstrated to be valid in circumstances
in which only two firms compete, there is perfect knowledge on the part
of sellers and buyers, and the behavior of buyers is hypersensitive.
Hypersensitive behavior refers to a situation in which buyers react to
the slightest difference between terms offered by different sellers; this is
contrasted with threshold-sensitive behavior which occurs where buyers
do not respond to differences in the terms offered by different sellers,
even though fully informed of the existence of these differences, until
terms differ by more than a certain amount. Increasing the number of
firms, introducing imperfect knowledge on the part of buyers or sellers,
or introducing threshold-sensitive behavior on the part of buyers can
change the conclusion that a firm's optimal strategy consists of imitating
its rivals.[6] Rather than engage in R&D investment like its rivals, for
example, a firm may rely upon advertising, and hope to keep abreast of
new technological developments by licensing new products.

Apart from the current behavior of its rivals, the profitability of different strategies considered by a firm will depend upon the extent to
which other firms react to such strategies. The profitability of any given
strategy will be lower, the more immediate the anticipated reaction.
The anticipated speed of reaction may, however, vary with the strategy
used; rivals might be expected to obtain information regarding some
types of strategy only after a longer lapse of time than in the case of
other strategies or, even though information is received as fast, it may
take rivals longer to fashion a reply. Decisions regarding expensive
R&D projects, for example, may take longer than decisions to increase
advertising outlays.

Significance of Product Differentiation in Price Theory

Elementary price theory includes in its list of market situations industries in which the product of different firms is differentiated. In

---

[6] See, for example, the article by N. E. Devletoglou, reference (5).

monopolistic competition, for example, each firm's demand curve is assumed to slope down because of product differentiation and the imperfect substitutability, in buyers' minds, of the products of different firms. In equilibrium, the price of each product exceeds the marginal cost of producing the product; in addition, the assumption of easy entry into the group means that the long-run equilibrium situation of the industry group involves tangency between the anticipated demand curve for each firm's product and the curve depicting the average cost (including normal profits) of producing and distributing the product, as shown in Figure 5–4.

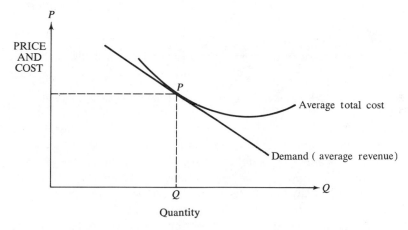

Figure 5–4   Long-Run Equilibrium of the Firm in Monopolistic Competition

Such an equilibrium situation has been contrasted unfavorably with the long-run equilibrium of a purely competitive industry on the grounds that in monopolistic competition there is excess capacity and inefficiency in the sense that if the total output of such an industry were concentrated in fewer firms, it could be produced at a lower cost in terms of money, and hence resources. In reply to this line of argument, some writers have pointed out that since average total cost (ATC) includes advertising outlays, each firm may be minimizing average production cost, as shown in Figure 5–5.

Even though firms are not minimizing average production costs, there is a more fundamental reply to the excess capacity argument. Assuming, for the moment, that the same total output would be demanded in the absence of product differentiation, concentration of total output into fewer firms necessarily results in elimination of some varieties of the product. The resulting output of the industry is, therefore, different from the output mix produced before, and it is impossible to compare the two

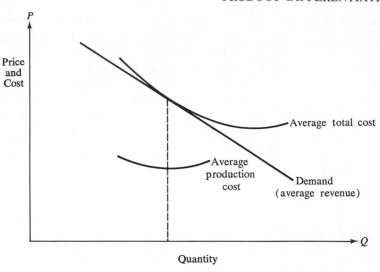

Figure 5–5   Production Costs versus Total Costs in Equilibrium

situations from the point of view of whether the "same" output is being produced more or less efficiently. One would require, instead, some criterion for comparing situations involving different mixes of output.

Moreover, total demand for the product(s) of an industry in which the products of individual firms are differentiated is not independent of production differentiation activities. Without product differentiation, the demand and cost conditions confronting firms will differ. One must avoid the temptation to conclude that the only thing that would be changed by absence of product differentiation is the slope of the individual firm's demand curve through the existing equilibrium price. Elimination of product differentiation implies elimination of efforts to achieve differentiation, such as advertising and R&D activities.

Product differentiation activities influence resource allocation apart from making the products of different firms imperfect substitutes for each other at a point in time. The *nature* of the products available at a given point in time will be influenced by (past) R&D activities, for example. Without R&D activities, the rate of introduction of new products and processes may differ, resulting in differences in the products available at any point in time. In addition, the *knowledge* possessed by buyers concerning products available will depend upon advertising activities. Advertising may provide information which enables buyers to choose the allocation of resources they prefer best.

Conventional price theory says nothing about the determinants of the level or characteristics of product differentiation activities undertaken by a firm. In price theory, product differentiation is simply assumed to exist in certain market structures, notably monopolistic competition and oligopoly with differentiated products, and is shown to have certain implications for pricing behavior. The main implication of the existence of product differentiation is that the price of a firm's product will exceed the marginal cost of producing and distributing the product.[7] A particular price-cost relationship is, however, quite compatible with numerous different levels of expenditure upon product differentiation activities, and any particular level of product differentiation outlay can be spent in numerous different ways. Price theory omits consideration of these matters entirely. In the section of this chapter entitled Product Differentiation Activity Mix, some of the factors influencing product differentiation have already been mentioned. Technological opportunity and characteristics of buyers' information in particular markets, for example, are relevant to the choice of product differentiation activity. Expectations regarding rivals' reactions, in addition, may be just as important in influencing the magnitude and character of product differentiation activities as they are in influencing pricing behavior. Although these expectations may be related to the number of firms in the market, the relationship is probably much more complex than in the case of pricing behavior, and a priori theorizing on this point is inconclusive. On the one hand, for example, larger numbers might be expected to lead to behavior which is heedless of rivals' reactions, involving a larger level of industry product differentiation activity than would be undertaken in similar circumstances if the industry were controlled by a smaller number of firms. On the other hand, larger numbers might be associated with pricing behavior leading to smaller profit margins and a smaller supply of funds to finance product differentiation activities. Another question concerns the extent to which the number of sellers in a market influences the character, as opposed to the magnitude, of product differentiation activities. Will, for example, the anticipated speed and extent of rivals' reactions be influenced by the type of product differentiation activity being contemplated by a firm? The answer to this question, and others concerning the relationship between seller concentration and product differentiation activities, can only be revealed by empirical evidence. Despite an increasing num-

---

[7] It must be stressed that absence of product differentiation does not guarantee equality of equilibrium industry price and marginal cost of production and distribution in firms in an industry with many firms. As demonstrated in the section of Chapter 4 entitled Importance of Assumed Reactions Rather than Numbers, equilibrium price-cost relationships involving price above marginal revenue (and hence above marginal cost, which equals marginal revenue in a profit-maximizing firm) are quite compatible with homogeneity of the industry's product, that is, with perfect substitutability of the products of different firms in the industry.

ber of statistical studies, the available empirical evidence is still scanty, and suggests no simple relationship between seller concentration and product differentiation. In view of the number of factors, other than concentration, which are likely to influence product differentiation, it would indeed be surprising to find a simple relationship, valid for all industries and at all times, between the number and size distribution of sellers in a market and their product differentiation activities.

Measurement of Product Differentiation

Product differentiation exists if the products of different firms in a particular industry are imperfect substitutes for each other from the point of view of buyers of those products. In Chapter 2, an industry was defined as a group of firms selling products which are close substitutes for each other from the point of view of buyers and sellers of the products. Product differentiation must, therefore, refer to a degree of difference which is less than that required to make the products of different firms members of different industries.

The drawing of industry boundaries in any practical case will greatly influence the degree of product differentiation one finds within the industry so defined. The wider the boundaries, the greater will be the degree of product differentiation observed, and vice versa.

How can the degree of product differentiation be measured once industry boundaries have been drawn? Counting the physical varieties, such as the number of differently flavored toothpastes, for example, is not always satisfactory. Product differentiation refers to differentiation in the minds of buyers, and this may be achieved by advertising activities despite the existence of only minor physical differences in the products of different firms. One possible measure of product differentiation would be obtained by using measures of cross-elasticity of demand between the products of firms that had already been grouped together into industries. The difficulties involved in obtaining such information have already been mentioned in Chapter 2.

Measuring the extent to which the products of different firms are imperfect substitutes for each other at a given point in time may, as already mentioned in the last section, be much less important than knowing the rate at which new products and processes are being created as a result of firms' efforts to differentiate their products through R&D activities. Alternatively, one may be interested in the determinants of product differentiation, or in the relationship between the level and type of a firm's product differentiation activities and other aspects of the firm's behavior. In these circumstances, it is appropriate to focus attention upon firm's *efforts* to differentiate their products as indicated by levels of advertising and R&D inputs employed, and upon the *results* of these efforts.

The firm's activities can be divided into investment in current production and product differentiation activities. The latter, in turn, can be divided into different product differentiation activities such as advertising and product policies, including R&D. There are likely to be problems associated with allocating a particular type of spending, or employees, or some other index of input, into these different categories. Some sales promotion activities are, for example, difficult to distinguish from current production activities. The outlays invested in inputs producing free samples of a particular product are just like investment in producing the same product for sale. However, giving away such products instead of selling them is aimed at shifting the demand schedule associated with the product, and the outlays should be classified as advertising outlays. Likewise, the measurement of R&D inputs, whether measured by expenditures, R&D personnel, or some other index, may often involve problems of classifying inputs.

There are even greater difficulties associated with measuring the output of firm's product differentiation activities than those encountered when attempting to measure inputs. For example, the following question has received much attention in recent statistical studies. Do increases in R&D inputs yield increasing returns, that is, more than proportionate increases in R&D output? The output of R&D activities is, however, a multidimensional concept; it includes increments of unpatentable new knowledge, patentable knowledge, patented knowledge, (patented) knowledge having commercial value, and so on. Unless these different concepts change in proportion to each other in response to changes in R&D input, the answer to the above question will depend upon the index of inventive output chosen. If one is interested in the flow of patentable knowledge, for example, patent applications, or patents granted, will not be a completely satisfactory index of this aspect of inventive output if the propensity to patent *patentable* knowledge varies between firms. Again, the benefits accruing from patented inventions, measured in terms of the value of sales of the invention or some other index of benefit, may vary from patent to patent, with the result that the number of patents granted will be a poor indicator of this dimension of R&D output.

Indexes of inventive output which have been employed in recent statistical studies of industrial research and development include the number of patent applications, patents granted, rankings of important inventions compiled by experts, and the value of the first two years' sales of a new product. These studies, however, frequently relate to different industries and very little attempt has been made to ascertain the extent to which different dimensions of R&D output are associated in particular industries. In the absence of this information, statements concerning the behavior of R&D output in response to changes in R&D input, or other aspects of firms' activities, must be interpreted with care.

The output of advertising activities is difficult to define, let alone measure, in a way that is operationally useful. It is clear that advertising is associated with the provision of information to buyers, and also that this may increase the sales of a firm's product. One cannot, however, measure in a very meaningful way how much information is provided to buyers by any particular level of advertising activities. Measuring the output of advertising in terms of its effect on a firm's sales would not be satisfactory; if competitors retaliate by increasing their own advertising efforts, for example, each firm might experience a negligible change in sales, yet buyers may be provided with more useful information than previously.

Further aspects of product differentiation activities, particularly the problems involved in attempting to define "ideal" performance in terms of product differentiation activities, and the relationship between "ideal" pricing behavior and these activities, are treated in Chapter 10, which deals with public policy towards industrial structure.

RECOMMENDED READINGS

1. Bain, J. S., *Barriers to New Competition* (Cambridge, Mass.: Harvard University Press, 1956) Chapter 4 and Appendix D.
2. Baldwin, W. L., "Contracted Research and the Case for Big Business," *Journal of Political Economy*, June 1962.
3. Buchanan, N. S., "Advertising Expenditures; a Suggested Treatment," *Journal of Political Economy*, August 1942. Also reprinted in W. Breit and H. M. Hochman (eds.) *Readings in Microeconomies* (New York: Holt, Rinehart and Winston, Inc., 1968.)
4. Comanor, W. S., "Research and Competitive Differentiation in the Pharmaceutical Industry in the U.S.," *Economica,* November 1964.
5. Devletoglou, N. E., "A Dissenting View of Duopoly and Spatial Competition," *Economica,* May 1965.
6. Dorfman, R., and P. O. Steiner, "Optimal Advertising and Optimal Quality," *American Economic Review*, December 1954.
7. Menge, J. A., "Style Change Costs as a Market Weapon," *Quarterly Journal of Economics*, November 1962.
8. Mueller, Dennis, "The Firm's Decision Process: An Econometric Investigation," *Quarterly Journal of Economics*, February 1967.

9. National Science Foundation, *Basic Research, Applied Research, and Development in Industry 1965*, NSF 67–12 (Washington, D.C.: U.S. Government Printing Office, 1967).

10. Stigler, G. J., "The Economics of Information," *Journal of Political Economy*, June 1961.

CHAPTER SIX

SELLER CONCENTRATION

Concentration and Behavior

Seller concentration refers to the number and size distribution of firms producing a particular type of output. Seller concentration has for a long time received more attention from economists and those concerned with public policy towards industry than any other single characteristic of industrial structure. This attention is motivated by a fundamental conviction that concentration is likely to play a large part in the determination of business behavior.

As already stressed in the second section of Chapter 4, analytically the number of firms in an industry is, itself, largely irrelevant as a determinant of pricing behavior. Given the number of firms in an industry, a different pattern of industry pricing behavior will result from different assumptions about rivals' reactions. Therefore, whether numbers influence behavior depends on whether numbers themselves influence each firm's *expectations regarding the behavior of its rivals*. Unless this expectation varies as the number of firms in a given industry changes, the industry behavior pattern will not change.

In price theory, a major distinction is made between markets in which the behavior of individual sellers is heedless of rivals' reactions (pure competition, monopoly, and monopolistic competition) and those in which individual sellers take into account rivals' reactions (oligopoly). Apart from monopoly, which is defined as a single firm supplying a particular market, these market situations are not defined in terms of the precise number of sellers involved in each case. There is no magic number of sellers which is supposed to divide oligopolistic from other market situations. The theoretical distinction is in qualitative terms; behavior which takes account of rivals' reactions will exist if one seller's behavior influences noticeably other sellers in the market. The extent to which the behavior of one firm will influence other firms noticeably may well be related to the number of firms in the market. The smaller the number of sellers, for example, the larger, on average, will be the fractions of a particular market supplied by individual sellers, and any given percentage gain in sales by one seller at the expense of the others results in a more noticeable loss to each of the others and is more likely to invite retaliation. There is, however, no single number of sellers which will in all circumstances distinguish oligopoly market situations from market situations characterized by behavior which is heedless of rivals' reactions. Whether a given sales loss to a rival will be noticed and attributed to the action of that rival will depend, for example, upon the general instability of industry sales due to other causes. Thus, a certain number of sellers sufficient to produce behavior which recognizes rivals' reactions in an industry with a very stable market might not do so in one with an unstable market.

Furthermore, within market situations in which rivals are influenced considerably by, and therefore take into account, each others' behavior, different patterns of behavior, related to differences in the degree of concentration, may occur. For these reasons, although theoretical considerations suggest the relevance of concentration to a study of pricing behavior, the existence and precise nature of such a relationship can only be established by empirical evidence.

Pricing is only one aspect of a firm's behavior. The relationship between concentration and price-cost relationships cannot fully describe the character of the competitive forces at work in a sector of the economy. It is equally important to know whether there is any relationship between concentration and other aspects of firms' behavior, such as advertising or R&D activities. Such knowledge is indispensable to the formulation of public policies towards business. Will, for example, reduced concentration mean better pricing performance, measured in terms of price-cost ratios, at the expense of less investment in R&D activities? If empirical evidence suggests that the answer to this question is affirmative, the policy maker must choose, and such a choice may not be easy. Even so, knowledge that choice is involved is likely to result in better policy measures than those taken without regard to all possible effects of a particular measure.

The argument that behavior depends upon the number and size distribution of competing sellers in a market does not, of course, deny the fact that other factors influence behavior. Also relevant may be whether demand for the industry's product is growing or declining, the rate of growth of industry demand over time, the character and speed of technological change, the characteristics of information flows in particular markets, the degree to which sellers operate in other markets, and the goals of individual firm policy. In view of the existence of differences in these other factors between industries, it would be surprising if a unique relationship between behavior and concentration were observed to exist in different industries. For this reason, studies of the relationship between seller concentration and various aspects of industry behavior should ideally take into account differences in these other factors, in order to attempt to isolate the relationship beween concentration and behavior.

Measurement of Concentration: Choice of Concentration Index

The degree of concentration, however it is measured for purposes of statistical study, is entirely dependent upon the industry definition used in the study. The broader the criterion used for grouping firms into industries, the larger will be the number of firms grouped together. Once an industry has been defined, and the number of firms in the industry is therefore determined, there are a number of different ways of measuring the degree of concentration. Several of these measures are related to the concept of the concentration curve shown in Figure 6–1.

The height of the concentration curve above any point x on the horizontal axis measures the percentage of the industry's total size

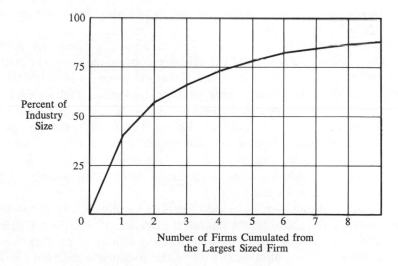

Figure 6–1 The Concentration Curve

accounted for by the largest x firms. Size of firms, and of the industry, may be measured either in terms of sales, net output, employment, assets, or some other index of size. Choice of the appropriate size variable is discussed in this chapter in the section entitled Measurement of Concentration: Choice of Size Variable. The horizontal axis in the concentration curve diagram measures the cumulative number of firms, starting with the largest. The concentration curve rises from left to right, reaching a maximum height of 100 percent at a point on the horizontal axis corresponding to the total number of firms in the industry. There will be one such curve for each industry in the economy, and each will refer to a specific period or point in time.

The index of concentration used most frequently, called the concentration ratio, measures the height of the concentration curve above a given point on the horizontal axis, which indicates the percentage of an industry's size accounted for by a given number of leading firms in the industry. In analyses of American data, the percentage of sales, net output, employment, or some other size variable, accounted for by the leading four firms, is frequently used; analyses of industrial concentration in Great Britain usually employ data for the three largest firms. The difference in the number of firms to which American and British ratios usually apply is the result of differences in the compilation of official statistics which have nothing to do with what is considered to be an appropriate measure of concentration.

Alternatively, instead of measuring the height of the concentration curve at a given horizontal distance from the origin, one can measure the horizontal distance to the curve at a given height. This measure of concentration yields the number of firms accounting for y percent of industry size.

These two types of concentration index depend on only one point on the concentration curve. If the relevant concentration curves intersect, comparison of concentration in different industries, or in a particular industry at different points in time, will yield different results, depending upon the point chosen, and an ambiguity exists as to which industry has the highest degree of concentration. In Figure 6–2, for example, industry A is more concentrated than industry B if concentration is measured by the percentage of industry size accounted for by the largest three firms, but industry B is more concentrated than industry A if ratios for six firms are used.

Whether concentration curves do intersect or not in any particular case can only be determined by empirical evidence. If they do not intersect, the ranking of industries by concentration at a given point in time, or the degree of concentration in a particular industry at different points in time, will not be influenced by the point on the concentration curve

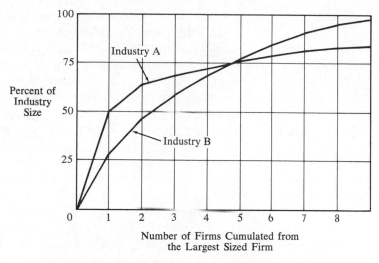

Figure 6–2 Intersecting Concentration Curves

chosen to represent the degree of concentration. This does not, however, necessarily imply that any point is as good as any other from the point of view of measuring concentration. The best measure of concentration is the measure which is most closely related to whatever aspect of industrial behavior one is interested in, and which therefore enables one to predict behavior most accurately. Agreement among ranks does not necessarily mean that the measures are good indicators of behavior; they may be equally poor indicators. On the other hand, if a concentration ratio which applies to four firms is more closely related to some aspect of industry behavior than a ratio for eight firms, the former is to be preferred to the latter, even though the ranking of concentration is independent of the number of firms used to calculate the concentration ratio.

The two types of concentration index discussed so far do not take into account the total number of firms in an industry. The value of the index may be identical for two industries, yet the behavior of the industries might differ significantly as a result of a difference in the remaining number of firms which are not taken into account by the index. It is likely, for example, that the behavior of an industry in which four firms account for 80 percent of total industry output and two firms supply the remaining 20 percent will differ from the behavior of an industry in which the remaining 20 percent is supplied by twenty other firms. Nor do these types of concentration index take into account the relative size of firms in the industry. This applies both to the relative size of the largest firms used in calculating the index, and to that of the remaining firms in the industry.

Measures of concentration which take account of the total number of firms in an industry are termed (summary) concentration indexes. Such indexes normally focus attention on the inequality of firm sizes in an industry, and are referred to as measures of inequality, or relative concentration, in contrast to absolute concentration measures of the type already discussed which are based on the concentration curve. Measures of relative concentration usually involve use of the Lorenz curve, which measures the cumulative percent of industry size accounted for by the various *percentages* of the number of firms in the industry. Apart from measuring cumulative percentage rather than cumulative number of firms on the horizontal axis, the only difference between the Lorenz curve and the concentration curve is that the former starts with the smallest firms in the industry, while the concentration curve starts with the largest firms.

The diagonal line which the Lorenz curve would follow if all firms in an industry were of equal size is referred to as the diagonal of equal distribution or line of absolute equality. The extent to which the Lorenz curve deviates from this line is an indicator of relative concentration; the area between the Lorenz curve and the diagonal of equal distribution is usually termed the area of concentration. Gini's concentration ratio is the ratio of the area of concentration to the total area below the diagonal of equal distribution and bounded by the axes of the diagram. If all firms in a particular industry were of equal size, the Gini coefficient would equal zero; the Lorenz curve would coincide with the diagonal of equal distribution, and there would be no area of concentration. At the other extreme, where one firm accounts for total industry size, the

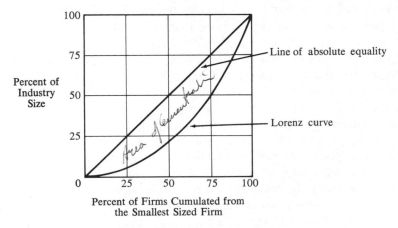

Figure 6–3 The Lorenz Curve

area of concentration coincides with the area under the diagonal of equal distribution and the Gini coefficient is equal to unity.

There are numerous other measures of relative concentration, either based on intercepts of the Lorenz curve or summarizing the whole size distribution. For example, the relative mean deviation intercept is found by drawing a positively sloped line parallel to the diagonal of equal distribution and tangent to a line showing the percentage of firms cumulated from the largest-sized firms. The point of intersection of this line with the vertical axis of the Lorenz curve diagram marks the relative mean deviation intercept, which is equal to one half the value of the relative mean deviation of firm sizes in the industry. The relative mean deviation equals the mean deviation of firm sizes in the industry, divided by the mean firm size, and is an index of inequality of firm size. Alternatively, another index of inequality, termed the Pietra ratio, is the ratio of the maximum triangle which can be inscribed in the area of concentration to the area under the diagonal of equal distribution and bounded by the axes of the Lorenz curve diagram. The Pietra ratio, it can be shown, is equal to the relative mean deviation intercept.

The Herfindahl summary index is another measure of concentration, and consists of the sum of squared firm sizes, all measured as a proportion of total industry size. Although this index is not based upon the Lorenz curve, it is a measure of inequality of firm sizes, or relative concentration. Thus, it can be shown that the index is equal to $(c^2 + 1)/n$, where c is the coefficient of variation of firm sizes and n is the number of firms in the industry. The coefficient of variation equals the standard deviation of firm sizes—a measure of inequality—divided by the mean firm size in the industry. The above formulation of the index enables the limiting values of the Herfindahl index to be easily interpreted. When all firms in an industry are of equal size, the standard deviation of firm sizes equals zero, and the Herfindahl index equals $1/n$, the reciprocal of the number of firms in the industry. If there is only one firm in an industry, the coefficient of variation is zero, and the index reaches a maximum value of unity.

Some empirical studies[1] have compared the ranking of concentration in different industries when using the Herfindahl index and concentration ratio measures. The evidence suggests that the use of any one of these three indexes would result in substantially the same ranking as any of the others. As already indicated, agreement among ranks does not necessarily mean that the measures are good indicators of behavior; they may be equally poor indicators. More important, however, is the

---

[1] See, for example, the study by G. Rosenbluth, reference (7).

point that the different indexes refer to different aspects of the size
distribution of firms in an industry, and should therefore be kept
analytically distinct from each other. Although absolute and relative
concentration are related, one of these concepts may change without
any change in the other, and they are capable of changing in opposite
directions. For these reasons, it is important to specify whether one is
referring to absolute or relative concentration when speaking of degrees
of, and changes in, concentration. Some writers[2] use the term concentration as synonymous with disparity of firm sizes within an industry,
so that the greater the disparity between the sizes of the largest and
smallest firms, the greater the degree of concentration. According to
this approach, an industry with size equally distributed among member
firms is not concentrated at all, even though the industry may consist
of very few firms and possesses a high degree of absolute concentration.
An industry which consists of five firms each with 20 percent of total
industry sales, for example, has a high degree of absolute concentration
since the top four firms account for 80 percent of sales, but relative
concentration is nil since each firm is equal in size as measured by their
respective sales. Similarly, it is possible for relative concentration to
decrease simultaneously with an increase in absolute concentration. A
merger which leaves the remaining firms in an industry closer in size
will reduce relative concentration or inequality, even though the degree
of absolute concentration may be increased by the reduction in the
number of firms in the industry.

Measures of relative concentration, stressing inequality of firm size,
have not been employed as frequently as absolute concentration
measures in studies of particular industries. Some economists have
argued that the latter type of measure is more directly relevant than the
former as an influence upon industry behavior. In support of this
argument it has been pointed out, for example, that two firms each
producing 50 percent of an industry's output yield the same value of the
Gini coefficient (zero) as 100 firms each supplying 1 percent of industry output, yet industry behavior will probably differ in the two
cases. This may be true, but the argument advanced by some economists,
that the number of sellers alone is important and that inequality of size
has no economic significance, must be rejected. It can be argued just as
plausibly on a priori grounds that inequality, not numbers, is more
important in influencing industry behavior in certain situations. Given
the number of firms in an industry, inequality of market share may play
an important part in determining whether particular firms in the industry

  [2] See, for example, S. J. Prais, "The Statistical Conditions for a Change in
Business Concentration," *Review of Economics & Statistics,* August 1958.

are capable of noticeably influencing other firms in the industry, and whether they take the latter into account in formulating policies. Compare, for example, two industries each with the same number of firms. In one industry the market shares are fairly evenly divided between firms and the effect of one firm's actions upon any other individual firm is not noticeable, so that individual firms in the industry act heedless of rivals' reactions. In the other industry, a few large firms produce the bulk of the industry's output, each firm aware of its influence on others and taking rivals' reactions into account, with a fringe of very small firms acting heedless of their influence upon other firms. The behavior of these two industries will probably differ although the number of firms in each industry is the same. In this example, an index of absolute concentration would yield different values for the two industries in question, as would an index of inequality. In other situations, however, differences in the disparity of firm sizes which have important implications for industry behavior may not be reflected by absolute concentration measures. The creation of a large firm through merger of smaller firms may challenge the market power of existing large firms and change behavior in the industry even though absolute concentration, measured by the share of the market supplied by the former leading firms, does not change.

Inequality of firm sizes may be just as important in determining behavior as the more conventional measures of absolute concentration. This has been recognized by the courts applying the United States' antitrust laws, and the concept of relative concentration is increasingly being resorted to as a judicial economic tool for appraising market structures.

The lack of application of relative concentration measures may be accounted for in part by the greater statistical and mathematical complexities of these measures. However, the argument that it may also reflect the greater data requirements of relative concentration measures is even less persuasive than the argument that absolute concentration is more relevant than relative concentration as a determinant of behavior. Some economists have argued, for example, that measures of inequality are more difficult to obtain because the number of firms in an industry is not usually known with any precision. If valid, this argument would also rule out the calculation of absolute concentration measures. After all, measures which indicate the percentage of total industry size accounted for by a specific number of firms can only be calculated if information regarding total industry size is available, and this requires information regarding the total number of firms in the industry, and their size. Conversely, if this information is available, it can be used for measures of relative concentration.

The list of possible concentration measures is by no means exhausted. As already indicated, concentration ratios say nothing about the distribution of industry size among the top three or four firms, nor between other firms in the industry. The Herfindahl index and other summary measures of inequality, likewise, do not distinguish clearly between these two aspects of concentration. These characteristics of the industry may influence behavior of the industry, and to discover whether this is the case some compromise measure of concentration involving both absolute and relative measures may be considered appropriate. An example of such a measure is the average size ratio, which is the ratio of the average size of a specific number of the leading firms to the average size of the remaining firms in an industry.

The question of which concentration index is best cannot be decided by resort to a priori arguments alone, but requires empirical investigation of the relationship between aspects of firm, or industry, behavior, and various concentration indexes. If concentration measures are to be used to indicate differences in behavior, the best index will be the one which is most closely related to whatever aspect of behavior one is interested in. Different indexes may be appropriate for different aspects of behavior. Ideally, it would be useful to use different concentration measures when undertaking any particular study, in order to discover whether the results of the study are influenced by the measures used. As already stressed, even though rankings of concentration do not vary with the index used, this need not mean that choice of index is irrelevant.

Measurement of Concentration: Choice of Size Variable

Apart from the question of which index of concentration is appropriate, there remains the question of whether to employ sales, net output, employment, assets, or some other size variable, as an index of firm, and industry, size. Although economic theory cannot offer much help in choosing between alternative indexes of concentration, theoretical considerations may help in choosing the most suitable quantity in terms of which to measure concentration.

If concentration measured in terms of different size variables were the same, choice of size variable would be irrelevant. Theoretical considerations suggest that this is unlikely, and empirical evidence supports the view that choice of size variable will influence measured concentration in many, if not most, industries. In many industries, absolute concentration measured by fixed capital assets is higher than concentration measured by sales, reflecting the fact that firms with larger sales have a larger ratio of assets to sales than firms with smaller sales. Large firms may use more capital and less labor per unit of final output than small firms, either because the relative price of capital equipment is lower for large firms than small, or because the optimal capital-labor ratio per unit of output increases with scale of output despite constant relative input prices. The higher degree of asset than sales concentration may, in other words, simply reflect a difference in the optimal capital-labor combination at higher levels of output. If this were the only factor underlying the observed relationship, however, one would expect employment concentration to be less than sales concentration. In some industries this is the case, but in others the relationship is reversed and both asset and employment concentration exceed sales concentration. In the latter industries, another influence, apart from the capital-labor ratio, is presumably at work, namely, vertical integration.

Even when the ratio of capital to labor is the same in firms with different levels of sales of a particular product, the ratio of assets (and employment) to sales will be higher in firms that are more vertically integrated than others, that is, in firms which themselves perform a greater number of preceding stages involved in the production of the final product. The use of assets, employment, or value added (sales minus purchases of inputs from other firms) as an index of firm size will mean that the resulting concentration measure reflects both horizontal and vertical aspects of firm size. The level of a firm's sales at a particular stage in the productive process refers to one dimension of firm size, and vertical integration to another, the number of successive stages involved in the production of the final product performed by the firm. Even when the capital-labor ratio per unit of output is the same in all firms, asset, employment, and value-added concentration will differ from sales concentration unless all firms in the industry in question are equally vertically integrated, and will reflect vertical aspects of firms' size in addition to horizontal aspects. Vertical integration may of course influence behavior just as much as horizontal size. However, horizontal size and vertical size, as well as their measurement, should be kept separate.

Finally, if the drawing of industry boundaries results in a situation in which a firm is a member of other industries in addition to the one studied, calculation of the proportion of the firm's total employment, or assets, actually "in" one of the industries involves an allocation of unspecialized inputs between different outputs, and therefore industries. This introduces an element of arbitrariness into the calculation of asset or employment concentration in any single industry, which can be avoided by using sales or value added as a measure of size.

Although asset, employment, sales, and net output concentration often differ within a given industry, the ranking of industries by concentration is often much the same no matter which standard of size is used. This will be the case if, for example, asset concentration tends to exceed sales concentration, which tends to exceed employment concentration, in all industries which are being studied. In these circumstances, analytical results which depend only upon rankings of concentration in different industries will not be greatly affected by the index of size used.

Determinants of Concentration

Attention has been focused upon concentration as a possible determinant of firm, and therefore industry, behavior. Concentration must be regarded not only as one of the factors influencing *current* behavior of firms, but also as one of the results of *previous* behavior. The degree of concentration is a *state* reached in a *process* of competition. For these reasons, even though concentration and various aspects of firms' behavior are observed to be closely related, the interpretation of such relationships may be difficult. Possible cause and effect may be very difficult to disentangle. For example, high advertising may, by causing high entry barriers, be a cause rather than a result of high concentration.

The degree of concentration existing in a particular industry at a point in time will be influenced by a number of factors. Firms' objectives, other structural features, and assumptions about other firms' behavior, whether established firms or potential entrants, will all be relevant in determining the degree of concentration.

Given a drive on the part of firms in an industry to exploit economies of scale and produce output levels which minimize the average cost of producing and distributing the industry's product, an upper limit to the number of firms in the industry will be determined by the size of the market in relation to the scale of output at which economies of scale become exhausted. Similarly, if there are diseconomies of scale beyond a certain scale of output, this will place a lower limit upon the number of firms supplying a given total market demand, provided always that the firms attempt to minimize unit costs. The upper and lower limits to the number of firms in the industry will only coincide if the long-run average cost curve of the industry in question were U shaped so that there were only one scale of output which minimized unit cost. In these circumstances the number of firms in an industry, and hence the degree of seller concentration in the industry, would be determined by scale economies and the size of the market. In practice, in many industries, there is a wide range of scales of output which minimize the unit cost of the industry's product, so that a number of different degrees of seller concentration are quite consistent with attempts to minimize unit costs in individual firms. Moreover, there is no reason why firms should necessarily attempt to produce a scale of output which minimizes unit cost; if a firm's objective is profit maximization, then, since profits are influenced by things in addition to unit cost, such as the price at which the firm can sell its output, for example, this objective may be achieved at scales of output which do not minimize unit cost. One reason, for example, why firms may not seek to expand output to levels which minimize average cost is that the anticipated reaction of other firms established in the industry is relevant to the price at which the firm expects to be able to sell its output. Firms producing scales of output lower than the scale which minimizes unit cost of the industry's product may feel no inclination to expand the level of their output by, say, cutting price, for fear of retaliation resulting in lower price and lower profits at a larger scale of output. Some industries tend to be less concentrated than scale economies alone would suggest.[3] On the other hand, firms may produce scales of output larger than those which minimize unit cost. The ability of firms in an industry to produce scales of output which do not minimize unit cost, and to sell at prices which cover these costs, depends to a large extent upon the existence of entry barriers into the industry concerned. If entry is easy, firms may be compelled to operate within the range of scales of output which minimize unit costs; this compulsion will be reduced as the height of entry barriers increases. Of course, even with high entry barriers, the behavior of established firms may compel operations at scales of output which minimize unit costs. Thus, if the established firms compete on a price basis, or on the basis of product differentiation activities which raise costs, firms producing scales of output which result in higher than minimum unit costs will be driven from the industry. The drive for profits may, however, lead to merger or collusion between independent firms in an industry rather than competition. The anticipated profits of a firm depend upon the firm's anticipations regarding its rivals' reactions. These can be eliminated by reducing the number of rivals, either by merger or collusion between independent firms. Opposing the concentration-increasing forces which result from entry barriers and a desire to eliminate competition within an industry, legal factors may in some countries operate to limit concentration. The antitrust laws of the United States are a prominent example in this connection. Similarly, market growth will influence concentration, because more rapid market growth normally implies lower barriers to entry and concentration in an industry will fall unless the established firms expand at the same rate as the market.

---

[3] See, for example, the evidence presented by L. W. Weiss in reference (13).

RECOMMENDED READINGS

1. Adelman, M. A., "The Measurement of Industrial Concentration," *Review of Economics and Statistics*, November 1951. Reprinted in R. B. Heflebower and G. W. Stocking (eds.), *Readings in Industrial Organization and Public Policy* (Homewood, Ill.: Richard D. Irwin, Inc., 1958). Published under the sponsorship of the American Economic Association. Also in H. J. Levin (ed.) *Business Organization and Public Policy* (New York: Holt, Rinehart and Winston, Inc., 1963).

2. Bain, J. S., "Relation of Profit Rate to Industry Concentration: American Manufacturing 1936–40," *Quarterly Journal of Economics*, August 1951.

3. Collins, N. R., and L. E. Preston, "Concentration and Price-Cost Margins in Food Manufacturing Industries," *Journal of Industrial Economics*, July 1966.

4. Comanor, W. S., and T. A. Wilson, "Advertising, Market Structure and Performance," *Review of Economics and Statistics*, November 1967.

5. Fuchs, V. R., "Integration, Concentration and Profits in Manufacturing Industries," *Quarterly Journal of Economics*, May 1961.

6. Mann, H. M., "Seller Concentration, Barriers to Entry, and Rates of Return in Thirty Industries, 1950–1960," *Review of Economics and Statistics*, August 1966.

7. Rosenbluth, G., "Measures of Concentration," in G. J. Stigler (ed.), *Business Concentration and Price Policy* (Princeton, N.J.: Princeton University Press, 1955).

8. Schwartzman, D., "The Effect of Monopoly on Price," *Journal of Political Economy*, August 1959.

9. Shepherd, W. G., "A Comparison of Industrial Concentration in the United States and Britain," *Review of Economics and Statistics*, February 1961.

10. ———, "Trends in Concentration in American Manufacturing Industries, 1947–1958," *Review of Economics and Statistics*, May 1964.

11. ———, "Changes in British Industrial Concentration, 1951–1958," *Oxford Economic Papers*, March 1966.

12. Weiss, L. W., "Average Concentration Ratios and Industrial Performance," *Journal of Industrial Economics*, July 1963.

13. ———, "The Survival Technique and the Extent of Sub-optimal Capacity," *Journal of Political Economy*, June 1964.

CHAPTER SEVEN

BARRIERS TO ENTRY

The term entry barriers refers to obstacles preventing new firms from engaging in the production of a particular category of output. Conventional price theory concludes that the price charged for the product of an industry characterized by perfectly easy entry cannot, in the long run, exceed average cost of production. Perfect ease of entry is said to exist if there are no barriers to entry into the industry concerned. If any entry barriers exist, price cannot in the long run exceed cost by more than the "height" of such barriers, it is argued. More recently, some economists have argued that the threat of potential entry may affect the price charged by firms already established in an industry and preserve the aforementioned relationship even in the short run, and despite the absence of actual entry. If valid, this line of reasoning elevates entry barriers, and in particular their height, to a position of great importance in determining price and output patterns in the economy as a whole.

We turn now to examine the role of entry barriers as a regulator of price, focusing particular attention upon the behavioral assumptions required to validate the above propositions.

Alternative Reactions to Entry

Entry into an industry shall be defined as the production, by a firm new to the industry, of a product that is a perfect substitute, in the minds of buyers, for the product of firms already established in the industry. This definition is quite consistent with variety in the physical

97

and other characteristics of the products of different firms in a given industry. It must also be emphasized that entry as defined is not accomplished if a firm previously outside an industry simply acquires the plant of an already established firm and operates it; that is, the mere change of ownership of existing plant capacity does not constitute entry. On the other hand, entry by a firm new to the industry need not necessarily involve the creation of a new firm; a firm already established in a particular industry may enter another industry if it builds capacity and adds an additional product to its product line.

Whether a decision maker will enter a particular industry or not depends upon the anticipated profitability of such a course of action. The profits anticipated by a potential entrant as a result of producing the product in question depend upon his cost conditions and upon the post-entry demand conditions anticipated by the firm for its product. These demand conditions, and therefore the profits anticipated by a potential entrant, depend upon the anticipated reaction of existing producers in the industry to entry. The greater the post-entry quantity of output produced by established firms, for example, the lower the price obtainable for any given quantity of the entrant's output. The many alternative reactions that are possible can each be viewed as a quantity of output which the existing firms can elect to produce after entry while reducing the price, or accepting reductions, to the extent required to enforce such an output policy. Diagrammatically, the potential entrant will then be confronted by a sloping demand curve which is the segment of the industry demand curve to the right of the *post-entry* quantity which the potential entrant expects existing firms to select, as shown in Figure 7–1.

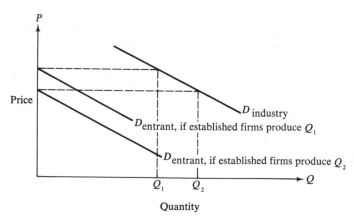

Figure 7–1   The Demand Curve Facing a Potential Entrant

Sylos Postulate

Much of the existing theory of entry is based upon the implicit or explicit assumption, sometimes referred to as the Sylos postulate, that potential entrants behave as though they expected existing producers in an industry to maintain their output at the pre-entry level in the face of entry, and that established firms do in fact behave in this manner if entry occurs.

Given the Sylos postulate, the potential entrant is confronted by a sloping demand curve which is the segment of the industry demand curve to the right of the *pre-entry* quantity produced by existing firms. The potential entrant will decide whether or not to enter the industry by comparing this demand curve with his own cost conditions. The entrant's costs must include the opportunity cost of the profit which can be earned in other industries; only if a firm can earn more profits in the industry being considered than can be earned elsewhere will the firm enter that industry.

Three main types of barrier to entry are customarily distinguished. First, preferences of buyers for the products of established firms as compared to those of new entrants. Such preferences can, however, always be overcome if the new entrant invests sufficiently in sales promotion activities, and the essence of preferences as a barrier to entry is that to secure comparably favorable price for any given quantity of output, the entrant would have to incur sales promotion costs per unit of output which are greater than those of established firms. In view of the definition of entry given earlier, preference barriers, if they exist, will emerge as a difference in the unit costs of established and potential entrant firms respectively. For this reason, preference barriers will be grouped for purposes of this analysis with the second major category of entry barrier, absolute cost advantages. Absolute cost advantages exist if the costs of established firms, at any comparable scale of output, are lower than those of potential entrants. Such advantages may result from the need of new entrants to overcome accumulated buyer preference for the product of established firms, or from other factors such as lower prices paid by established firms for inputs or investment funds. The third major type of entry barrier is economies of scale, resulting in a declining long-run average cost curve for the product in question. Some economists list legal barriers as a fourth type of entry barrier, while others would not distinguish them as a separate type of barrier, preferring instead to include the various types of legal barrier under the three main categories of barrier already listed. For example, patents giving established firms exclusive rights over strategic productive techniques or product designs may place potential entrants at a disadvantage in cost if they must use more costly techniques or must pay royalties for use of the patented technique or product. Such legal barriers may therefore be included with absolute cost barriers. Other legal barriers, however, such as laws prohibiting entry absolutely, or requiring operators to obtain government granted licenses, may not be reflected in costs, and must be listed as a separate category of entry barrier. The succeeding analysis confines itself to the three main categories of barrier already listed.

The presence of absolute cost differences, or scale economies, is not by itself sufficient to guarantee a barrier to entry—entry will occur despite such factors, provided that the entrant's anticipated demand conditions result in a situation in which the entrant expects to be able to make a profit. This is the case, for example, in both situations shown in Figure 7–2. The curves labeled ATC entrant and ATC established depict, respectively, the average cost curves of a potential entrant and an established firm.

Given the Sylos postulate, the position of the demand curve confronting a potential entrant is determined by the pre-entry price and output of established firms. Where absolute cost differences exist, if the pre-entry price exceeds the average cost in established firms by more than the difference in average cost between potential entrant and established firms, the entrant's demand curve will be above his cost curve (in view of the assumed constancy of established firms' output at the pre-entry level) and entry will occur since the entrant expects to make a profit. Entry will lower market price if established firms do in fact behave in the expected manner and attempt to maintain output at the pre-entry level. Entry will not occur if the pre-entry price exceeds cost in established firms by less than the difference in average cost between

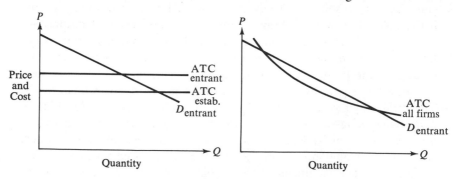

Figure 7–2   Entry Despite Absolute Cost Differences
and Scale Economies

potential entrant and established firms, for in such circumstances, given
the Sylos postulate, the entrant's anticipated demand curve will be
below his cost curve. The greater the difference in absolute costs of
established firms and potential entrant the greater the amount by which
industry price can exceed cost of established firms without inducing
entry. If the extent to which industry price can exceed average cost in
established firms is used as a measure of the height of entry barriers, the
height of absolute cost entry barriers, given the Sylos postulate, is
measured by the distance xy in Figure 7–3(a). The distance equals precisely the absolute cost difference between established firms and potential
entrants.

If scale economies exist, the maximum amount by which price can
exceed average cost without inducing entry, given the Sylos postulate,
is determined by the size of the market, the elasticity of market demand
at any price, the scale at which economies of scale are exhausted and the
rate at which average cost declines. The height of the scale economies
barrier to entry is measured by the distance vw in Figure 7–3(b).

If both types of entry barrier exist, the maximum amount by which
price can exceed average cost without inducing entry, given the Sylos
postulate, will be determined by the height of the larger of the two
barriers.

The following propositions are valid if firms behave in accordance
with the Sylos postulate:

1. Entry will occur if price exceeds average cost of the marginal,
or least efficient, established firm by more than an amount that is directly
related to the magnitude of scale economies and absolute cost differences
between established firms and new entrant, and price cannot exceed cost
by more than this amount in the long run, though it may do so in the
short run, that is, until entry has occurred.

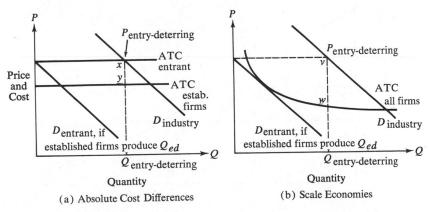

Figure 7–3 Maximum Price-Cost Differences under the Sylos Postulate

2. If existing producers in an industry try to deter potential entrants, this relationship between price and cost will be preserved even in the short run. That is, in order to deter entry, existing producers must charge a price which does not exceed average cost by more than the height of scale economy or absolute cost entry barriers. Only if such a price is set will entry seem unprofitable to potential entrants, provided that they expect existing firms to keep their output levels constant in the face of entry.

Whether producers will attempt to deter potential entrants depends upon the relative profitability of charging a short-run profit-maximizing price, and pricing to deter entry. The relative profitability of the two courses of action depends primarily on the anticipated lapse of time before entry will occur in response to existing firms charging a price higher than the entry-deterring price. This proposition can be demonstrated with the aid of Figure 7–4. Diagrammatically, assuming the existence of absolute cost barriers and ignoring discounting of more distant profits, the choice is between profits equal to area *ACEF*, obtained by pricing to deter entry, and profits equal to

$$\frac{\text{area ABHG} \times \left(\begin{array}{c}\text{period before}\\\text{entry occurs}\end{array}\right) + \text{area ABDC} \times \left(\begin{array}{c}\text{period after}\\\text{entry occurs}\end{array}\right)}{\text{total period to which the industry demand curve applies}}$$

If entry in response to a price higher than the entry-deterring price is instantaneous, for example, profits from charging a price higher than the entry-deterring price are equal to area *ABDC*, and producers will

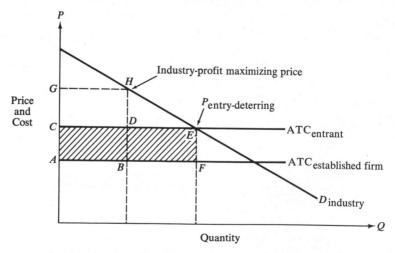

Figure 7–4   Pricing to Deter Entry under the Sylos Postulate

adopt the alternative course of action, and price to deter entry. At the other extreme, if entry does not occur before the end of the period to which the industry demand curve applies, profits from charging a short-run profit maximizing price are area *ABHG*, and existing firms in the industry will not price to deter entry.

Consequences of Alternative Reactions

The propositions in the preceding section cease to be valid if potential entrants do not assume that established firms will maintain their output at the pre-entry level. It is the *post-entry* output of existing firms anticipated by potential entrants that determines the anticipated price at which the entrant can sell any given output level. *Pre-entry* price and quantity sold are themselves generally irrelevant as far as the potential entrant is concerned, and only become relevant to the entry decision in special cases in which entrants assume that the post-entry quantity supplied by established firms will equal the pre-entry quantity. It is not true, as is often stated in elementary price theory texts, that the relevant question for a new entrant is whether existing firms are charging prices at which the new entrant can make above normal profits. Rather, it is whether the reaction of established firms to entry will result in a *post-entry* price which permits the entrant to make above normal profits.

The post-entry quantity supplied by existing firms which will deter entrants (since it will imply a post-entry market price which will not enable the entrant to cover costs at any level of output), and the entry-deterring price, are uniquely determined by long-run demand and cost functions of the industry, as explained in the previous section. However, entry will not necessarily occur if pre-entry price exceeds the entry-deterring price so determined. If, for example, the potential entrant expects established firms to produce a post-entry quantity which will not permit the entrant to cover his costs, entry will not occur irrespective of the pre-entry price that is being charged by established firms. The size of absolute cost differences and scale economies relative to the size of total market demand no longer place a limit on the amount by which price can permanently exceed unit cost in the established firms, even in the long run.

Moreover, if the pre-entry price charged by established firms has no influence on the entrant's decision, it follows that charging a price lower than the industry profit-maximizing price, in order to deter entry, cannot possibly be an optimal strategy from the point of view of established firms with profit-maximizing objectives. This conclusion is obvious in the example quoted in the preceding paragraph in which entry does not take place, for in this event the established firms are forgoing profits if they charge a price other than the price which maximizes industry profit. It is perhaps less obvious, but equally true, even if potential entrants decide to enter the industry because they expect the reaction of existing producers to entry will be such as to permit the entrant to earn a profit. If entry is independent of pre-entry price charged by existing firms, the post-entry profits of existing firms will be the same whether or not those firms charged a pre-entry price that maximizes industry profits in the pre-entry period; therefore, pricing to deter entry and earning pre-entry profits below the maximum possible level must lower the total profits of firms practicing such a policy relative to the profits that can be earned if potential entry is ignored. Limit pricing will not be the most profitable course of action for existing producers unless they believe that potential entrants expect established firms to attempt to maintain their output at the pre-entry level in the face of entry.

The question remains, what grounds are there for assuming that potential entrants expect established firms to attempt to maintain output at the pre-entry level, or that established firms expect them to behave in this way? Some economists have suggested that this is the policy that is most unfavorable to new entrants. In the absence of some constraint which prevents established firms from increasing the level of their output in response to entry, however, this conclusion is not warranted. (Such a constraint could be provided, for example, by an antitrust policy which would regard increases in output by established firms in response to entry as a restrictive practice.) If existing firms increase their output after entry has occurred, the price which the entrant can obtain for any given quantity of output is lower than if existing firms maintained their output at the pre-entry level. Thus, by increasing output after entry has occurred, established firms can force losses upon the entrant firm. There is no such thing as the most unfavorable policy for entrants, short of driving price down to zero. From the point of view of potential entrants, the most unfavorable policy which established firms are likely to consider adopting is surely the policy of trying to deter entrant firms by supplying a post-entry quantity which drives market price down below the entrant firm's costs. There is, however, no more reason why potential entrants should expect established firms to react in this way in all circumstances than there is reason to believe that they will attempt to maintain output constant in all circumstances, as the Sylos postulate assumes. In atomistic market structures, to be sure, the behavior of potential entrants will very likely correspond to the Sylos postulate. Under pure competition or monopolistic competition, for example, no individual established seller will take account of entry, any more than it will take account of the behavior of its existing rivals. By definition, in such markets the actions of any individual seller, whether established firm or new entrant, will have no noticeable effect upon other sellers, and will not, therefore, provoke any reaction. Therefore, the Sylos postulate is a valid description of the behavior of potential entrants considering entering an atomistic industry. The situation is different in oligopolistic industries. In such industries, individual established firms are by definition affected by and aware of the actions of other firms, whether established firms or new entrants, and may be expected to react by potential entrants. The exact nature of the reaction, however, cannot be determined by a priori reasoning. In the final analysis, how potential entrants actually behave, or how established firms believe them to behave, is a matter for empirical investigation.

Before we leave the subject of the determinants of potential entrants' behavior, it is necessary to mention briefly one other possible barrier to entry. Thus far it has been pointed out that if the entrant's anticipated demand and cost conditions indicate that a profit can be made, entry will occur. In order to enter, however, the firm must, in addition, have sufficient money capital to purchase the inputs required to produce the level of output which it expects to be able to sell at a profit. If the cost of investment funds is higher for a potential entrant than for established firms, this will be reflected as an absolute cost difference and will therefore be covered by the analysis of absolute cost barriers. If, however, a potential entrant is unable to obtain funds at any price, the capital requirements barrier will not be reflected in the entrant's cost curves and must therefore be treated as a separate category of entry barrier. The belief is widely held that the requirement of a large amount of liquid funds for investment by an entrant firm constitutes some sort of barrier to its entry. While the argument the potential entrants simply cannot raise enough money (presumably at any price) to finance entry, or that established firms can raise money more easily and cheaply than potential entrants, is plausible if the new entrant is a new firm setting up business for the first time, it is less so if one considers the possible entry of a large going business concern into a new industry.

Actual Entry and Level of Industry Price and Output

Although the height of entry barriers will not place a limit on the amount by which price can exceed average cost, even in the long run, if potential entrants expect entry-deterring behavior by established firms after entry has occurred, entry will occur whenever potential entrants expect the reaction of established firms will permit entrants to make profits.

The question remains, will *actual* entry itself lower market price and place a limit on the amount by which price can exceed average cost in the long run?

The answer to this question depends on how established firms and new entrants behave after entry has taken place. If established firms attempt to maintain their output at the pre-entry level, entry will drive down the market price, but the resulting market price may continue to exceed average cost by more than the height of absolute cost and scale economy entry barriers, Figure 7–5 demonstrates.

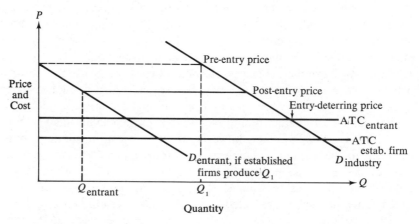

Figure 7–5   The Effects of Actual Entry on Industry Price and Output

Only if additional entry occurs will market price be driven down further, and this depends on whether new potential entrants expect the established firms to continue to react to entry by attempting to maintain output at the pre-entry level.

If, contrary to the expectations of new entrants, established firms try to deter entry by increasing output, market price will be driven down at least until it exceeds cost by no more than the height of entry barriers until the entrant has been eliminated, but can then be raised again unless and until entry occurs again. It can hardly be argued that further entry will prevent price being raised again, unless entrants ignore the previous behavior of established firms in response to entry.

The third possibility is that existing firms may reduce their output in the face of entry, and that industry price continues to exceed cost by more than the height of entry barriers, perhaps even remaining unchanged despite the occurrence of entry and despite the absence of any collusion between firms in the industry. This possibility can be illustrated by the following example employing the extreme assumption that there are no scale economy or absolute cost barriers to entry into a particular industry. If each firm in an industry assumes that any price it charges will be matched by all other firms in the industry, each firm's demand curve will be a fraction of the industry demand curve, the size of the fraction determined by the anticipated share of market demand accruing to the firm if all firms charge the same price for the same product. Figure 7–6 illustrates this proposition in the case of a linear market demand curve.

Increases in the number of firms in the industry will cause the subjective demand curve assuming price matching of each established firm to pivot down without changing the intercept of that curve. Since, by definition, there are no economies of scale and no absolute cost differences, the cost curves of established and newly entered firms will be identical, and marginal cost of production and distribution will be constant.

With linear cost and demand functions, the price which maximizes a firm's profits depends only on the intercept of the demand curve and on marginal cost of production and distribution.[1] In the absence of scale economies, marginal cost is by definition constant; further, the entry of an additional firm leaves the intercept of an established firm's demand curve assuming price matching unchanged. Therefore, if the industry demand curve is linear (and firms expect rivals to behave as postulated), it follows that entry will leave the profit-maximizing price of each established firm unchanged. Finally, since the new entrant's cost conditions are identical with those of established firms, and its demand curve is linear with the same intercept as the demand curve of established firms, the profit maximizing new entrant will charge the same price as established firms. In these circumstances, entry does not change industry price and output, but merely changes the number of firms producing that output—an output which maximizes industry profits.

---

[1] For example, with the demand function $p = a - bq$
and the total cost function $C = cq + K$
Profit $= aq - bq^2 - cq - K$
For maximum profit, $\dfrac{dP}{dq} = 0$
Therefore, $a - 2bq - c = 0$, or $q = \dfrac{a - c}{2b}$

Substituting the profit-maximizing quantity into the demand function we obtain the profit-maximizing price as a function of its determinants, as follows:

$$p = a - b\,\frac{(a - c)}{2b} = \frac{2a - a + c}{2} = \frac{a + c}{2}$$

Thus, the profit-maximizing price depends solely on c, the marginal cost of production, and a, the y intercept of the demand curve.

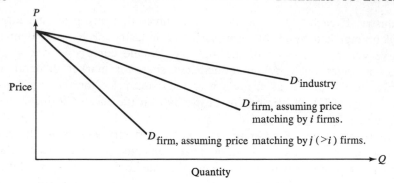

Figure 7–6 Entry with Price Matching

The preceding example emphasizes that the relationship between industry price and unit cost depends upon the behavior of individual firms established in the industry, and that this behavior can take a number of different forms. Even in the absence of entry barriers, actual entry into the industry will not necessarily drive price down to equality with unit cost unless firms in the industry ignore each others' behavior in deciding upon their individual policies. The example also shows that the number of firms in an industry is only relevant to explaining industry behavior insofar as it influences expectations about rivals' behavior.

If entry barriers exist, it is still possible for industry price to remain unchanged despite the entry of additional firms into the industry. For example, with absolute cost barriers added to the previous example, although the price which maximizes profits, given the assumption of price matching by all firms, remains unchanged for established firms, this price will be higher for new entrants. However, the entrant may passively accept the price which maximizes established firms' profits, given entry, believing that established firms are unlikely to match a higher price set by the entrant, although believing that established firms will very likely match any attempt to undercut them. Given this expectation, passive acceptance of the price set by established firms may be the most profitable course of action for an entrant.

Theory of Entry as an Extension of Oligopoly Theory

Two main points emerge from the preceding discussion. First, whether entry into an industry will occur depends upon the post-entry behavior of established firms anticipated by potential entrants. Such behavior can

take various alternative forms, each of which implies a different anticipated level of profits accruing to the entrant and which need not necessarily correspond to the pre-entry behavior of established firms. Second,
the effect of entry on industry price and output depends upon the actual
post-entry behavior of firms in the industry including any new entrants,
and varies with the assumptions regarding rivals' reactions made by the
individual firms in the industry after entry has occurred.

In each case, the analogy between the theory of entry and the
oligopoly situation of traditional price theory should be apparent to
the reader. Oligopoly theory deals with firms' behavior, taking into
account the firms' expectations regarding the behavior of other firms
already producing the product. As for the effect of potential entry on
the behavior of established firms, entry theory merely extends the
number of firms considered by established firms in their policy making,
to firms *not already in the group* who may react to the established
firms' policies by entering the industry.

Whereas the behavior of potential entrants depends upon how they
expect established firms to react to entry, the behavior of established
firms depends upon how established firms *think* potential entrants
expect them to react to entry. It must be stressed that in order to
establish any a priori link between the behavior of established firms and
the threat of potential entry, it is necessary to show that established
firms believe potential entrants to be influenced by the *pre-entry* behavior of established firms. Since the profitability of entry depends upon
the *post-entry* behavior of established firms anticipated by potential
entrants, this virtually amounts to a need to show that potential entrants
expect the pre-entry and post-entry behavior of established firms to be
the same. Theories which attempt to show that behavior of established
firms is influenced by the threat of potential entry stand or fall according
to whether established firms believe that the Sylos postulate is an accurate description of potential entrants' behavior.

Measuring Entry Barriers

The height of entry barriers into an industry will be reflected by the
extent to which price can exceed average cost in established firms
without inducing entry. In the section of this chapter entitled Sylos
Postulate, it was demonstrated that, given the Sylos postulate, price
could not, in the long run, exceed average cost by more than an amount
which is directly related to scale economies and absolute cost differences
between established firms and potential entrants. In these circumstances
information concerning scale economies and absolute cost differences

alone would enable one to rank industries in terms of the height of
entry barriers. If, however, potential entrant firms' behavior does not
correspond to the Sylos postulate, the amount by which price can exceed cost without inducing entry bears no direct relationship to scale
economies and absolute cost differences. If potential entrants anticipate
entry-deterring behavior by established firms, price may exceed average
cost in established firms by much more than absolute cost differences or
scale economies alone would suggest. It follows that one can then no
longer judge the height of entry barriers merely by reference to scale
economies and absolute cost differences. In addition, since the height of
the barrier to entry is also a function of the conjectures of potential entrants concerning the reactions of established firms to their entry, some
kind of index is required which would indicate the reaction to entry
anticipated by potential entrants.

Even without such an index, however, there are certain other features
of an industry which indicate the ease or difficulty of entry, for example
the extent to which industry demand is increasing over time. In general,
entry will be easier if industry demand is increasing, for a potential
entrant will be able to enter the industry without encroaching upon the
markets of existing firms, and without necessitating a decline in the
profitability of pre-entry levels of output produced by existing firms.

Finally, our discussion of entry barriers has been conducted on the
assumption of a fixed and unchanging technology. If the cost curves of
potential entrant and established firms differed, it was because of higher
prices paid for inputs, or less efficient inputs, used by the potential
entrant. In a world of changing technology, entry into an industry may
of course be gained through the use of some new technology. There is
no a priori reason why established firms in an industry should have a
monopoly of the rate of change of technological knowledge applicable
to the industry. If, as a result of their own technological efforts, potential
entrants obtain an absolute cost advantage over established firms, entry
will probably occur irrespective of the anticipated reaction of established
firms.

RECOMMENDED READINGS

1. Bain, J. S., "A Note on Pricing in Monopoly and Oligopoly," *American Economic Review*, March 1949.
2. ———, "Conditions of Entry and the Emergence of Monopoly," in
   E. H. Chamberlin (ed.) *Monopoly and Competition and their Regu-
   lation* (London: Macmillan & Co., Ltd., 1954) pp. 215–241.
3. ———, *Barriers to New Competition* (Cambridge, Mass.: Harvard
   University Press, 1956.).

4. Comanor, W. S., and T. A. Wilson, "Advertising, Market Structure and Performance," *Review of Economics and Statistics*, November 1967.

5. Hines, H., "Effectiveness of 'Entry' by Already Established Firms," *Quarterly Journal of Economics*, February 1957.

6. Johns, B. L., "Barriers to Entry in a Dynamic Setting," *Journal of Industrial Economics*, November 1962.

7. Mann, H. M., "Seller Concentration, Barriers to Entry, and Rates of Return in Thirty Industries, 1950–1960," *Review of Economics and Statistics*, August 1966.

8. Modigliani, F., "New Developments on the Oligopoly Front," *Journal of Political Economy*, June 1958.

9. Osborne, D. K., "The Role of Entry in Oligopoly Theory," *Journal of Political Economy*, August 1964.

10. Sylos-Labini, P., *Oligopoly and Technical Progress* (Cambridge, Mass.: Harvard University Press, 1962).

11. Wenders, J. T., "Entry and Monopoly Pricing," *Journal of Political Economy*, October 1967.

CHAPTER EIGHT

VERTICAL INTEGRATION

The degree of vertical integration refers to a state of industrial organization; it refers to the extent to which successive stages involved in the production of a particular product or service are performed by different firms, or the converse, the extent to which a firm performs different successive stages in the production of a particular product. Vertical integration is also used to describe the action of a firm in acquiring or constructing facilities for carrying out productive stages which formerly either preceded or succeeded its original productive activities. Backward and forward vertical integration refer to the acquisition of preceding or succeeding stages respectively. Where two existing firms merge, and the decision is a joint one, whether the situation is one of backward or forward vertical integration depends upon the point of view. One can also distinguish partial from complete vertical integration, considering any two successive stages. In the former case, a firm may still use the market for acquiring part of its supplies, or for the disposal of part of its output, producing only part of its total requirements of a particular input, or processing further only part of its output at an earlier stage.

If one defines the output of different stages as different products, vertical integration is an aspect of diversification. However, the considerations motivating firms to diversify in the sense of vertical integration, and the results, differ in a number of respects from the considerations motivating diversification in the sense of producing vertically unrelated outputs. In this book, the term diversification refers only to activities that are not vertically related.

113

Determinants of Vertical Integration

In discussing the determinants of vertical integration we shall first consider the motives prompting backward integration.

Consider a firm purchasing inputs and combining these to produce a particular final product. Some of the inputs purchased may themselves be the final product or service of firms at an earlier stage of the productive process. Backward integration by the firm at the later stage may reduce the cost of producing the firm's final product, for one or both of the following reasons. First, even though the cost of performing each successive stage remains unchanged, or increases, profits included in the price formerly paid to firms selling the product of earlier stages can be avoided, and on balance the cost of obtaining the output of the earlier stage may be reduced. Second, and perhaps more important, vertical integration may mean that certain costs of using the market are avoided, thereby reducing the cost of performing the successive stages when these are combined under a single managerial supervision. Costs of using the market may fall on one or both of two separate firms performing vertically related productive processes, and can take many different forms. For example, a firm at an earlier stage may engage in advertising or other sales promotion activities aimed at securing the custom of firms at the later stage. The second stage of a vertically integrated firm provides, on the other hand, a certain market for the output of the firm's first stage. Alternatively, an unintegrated firm performing a later stage may keep a greater level of stocks of the product of the earlier stage than if it controls the earlier stage itself and can therefore coordinate the flow of output between different stages. As a final example, if each successive stage in the production of a particular final product requires that the output of the previous stage be heated, the cost of the final product may be reduced by performing the successive operations before cooling of intermediate outputs takes place.

There are many other examples of the way in which costs of using the market can be avoided by vertical integration. However, vertical integration may result in additional costs which would not be present in the unintegrated firms. Coordinating two successive stages may, for example, require administrative inputs over and above those required to run the two separate stages, resulting in additional administrative costs per unit of final output. Any such costs of vertical integration must be compared with the saving in costs of using the market plus intermediate profit payments avoided, in order to determine whether backward vertical integration will reduce costs of the final product.

By reducing the cost of producing the integrating firm's final product,

backward vertical integration may contribute to a number of different objectives. A firm with profit-maximizing objectives will integrate backwards if this reduces the total cost of producing any given level of its final product for, given the demand conditions for its final product, a reduction in cost at any level of output represents an increase in profit at that level of output.

It must be stressed that a profit-maximizing firm may not produce the same level of final output after integration. As explained in this chapter in the section entitled Vertical Integration and the Level of Output, the scale of the firm's final output will remain unchanged if the cost saving attributable to vertical integration is the same at all levels of output. In this case the slope of the firm's total cost curve, and therefore marginal cost of final output, remains unchanged, as does marginal revenue if demand conditions at the final stage are constant. If the cost saving decreases with scale of final output, the profit-maximizing level of final output will decrease as a result of vertical integration; the reverse is true if the cost saving increases with scale of final output.

A firm with sales-revenue-maximizing objectives will also integrate backwards provided that the cost of the final product is thereby reduced. The act of backward vertical integration itself does not increase sales revenue. However, it was pointed out in Chapter 1 that a sales revenue maximizer is constrained by the need to make some profits, either to finance current dividend payments or growth of output and sales revenue in the next period. If the unintegrated sales revenue maximizer is producing a level of final output which satisfies this constraint, a reduction in the cost of that output and consequent increase in profits will permit sales revenues to be increased. In contrast to the profit maximizer, backward vertical integration by a sales revenue maximizer will always lead to an increase in the scale of final output because, given demand conditions for the final product, increases in sales revenue can only be obtained by increasing the scale of output, assuming of course that price elasticity of demand for the final product exceeds unity so that marginal revenue is positive.

Finally, consider a firm which desires to maximize the growth rate of some aspect of the firm's operations. In Chapter 1 it was pointed out that growth depends upon profits, because profits are required either to finance growth internally, or to obtain additional external finance. If backward vertical integration increases profits, it will increase the maximum attainable growth rate of the firm; therefore, a growth rate maximizer will also integrate if this reduces the cost of producing its final product.

We have been discussing the considerations motivating a firm to integrate backwards, pointing out that, given the demand conditions for its final product, any move that reduced the cost of a given output level must increase the profits associated with that output level. The reduction in cost may be the result of eliminating an intermediate profit, or may also include a reduction in the actual costs of performing successive productive stages when these are combined under a single managerial supervision.

Forward vertical integration may take place for reasons similar to those motivating backward vertical integration. If the cost of performing successive stages is not affected, the integrating firm will be able to add to the profits from performing its original stage, the profits associated with performing the later stage, which depend upon the cost and demand conditions associated with the later stage. Integration may, in addition, reduce the cost of performing the combined stages by eliminating costs of using the market; any such reduction will represent an additional increase in profits over and above the profit that can be earned by unintegrated firms performing the later stage. Against these two sources of increased profit must be set any costs of vertical integration, in order to determine whether forward vertical integration is on balance profitable.

A firm may integrate forward partially in order to separate the market for the product of its original stage and increase the firm's profits by enabling it to discriminate on a price basis. In the absence of vertical integration, the possibility of resale between different sectors of the market for the unintegrated firm's product may prevent price discrimination even though it would be profitable. Consider, for example, a firm selling to buyers located in two different geographical areas. For simplicity, assume that transportation costs between seller and each area are the same. If the elasticity of demand for the product at any particular price differs in the two areas, the firm could earn more profit if it charges a different price for its product in each area than by charging the same price in each area. Any attempt to charge a different mill price to buyers in the different areas will, however, tend to be thwarted by resale from low-price to high-price buyers. In order to separate the markets and prevent such resale, the firm could integrate forward and perform also the transportation stage. In these circumstances, the prices charged in the two areas can differ by any amount up to the cost of transporting the product direct between the two areas before resale from low-price to high-price area becomes profitable. As indicated in Chapter 4 in the section entitled Delivered Pricing versus Mill Pricing, the seller need not necessarily perform the transportation function himself in order to separate the market; an alternative method of separating the market would be to charge delivered prices while hiring the services of some independent firm to transport the product from seller to buyers.

The fact that a firm expects vertical integration to increase its profits is not, by itself, sufficient to result in integration. Performing productive processes that are linked to each other vertically requires the investment of capital in the productive activities carried out at each stage. Differences in vertical integration between firms may reflect differences in the supply of capital available to the firms rather than differences in the expected profitability of vertical integration. Finally, even though a firm has sufficient capital to meet the requirements of vertical integration, the firm will not integrate unless the profit per unit of capital invested in performing an additional stage exceeds the return that could be earned if the capital were invested elsewhere, including additional investment in diversification or horizontal growth in existing markets. Only if vertical growth achieves the firm's objectives better than these other forms of expansion will the firm select this form of investment. Thus, for example, even though a firm can perform a stage of production preceding or succeeding its current operations just as efficiently as firms currently performing the stage, and can therefore cut out the middleman's profit by integrating, there will be no incentive to do so if the firms currently performing that stage are earning only normal profits.

Vertical Integration and Level of Output

In this section we shall consider the effect of vertical integration, that is, the combining under one decision-making unit of two or more formerly independent successive stages involved in the production of a particular product, on the price and output of the final product. It will be assumed, for the present, that conditions of demand for the final product remain unchanged, and that firms wish to maximize profits.

If vertical integration leaves the cost conditions associated with each stage in the productive process unchanged, then vertical integration will not change the price and level of output of the final product in each of the three following cases:

1. Vertical integration between two firms at successive purely competitive stages.
2. Vertical integration between a monopoly at one stage and a single firm at another purely competitive stage.
3. Vertical integration between a monopoly at one stage and all of the firms at a purely competitive stage.

In cases 1 and 2, combined firm profits will not, for example, be increased if the first stage of the combined firm sells its output to the second stage at a lower price than before integration. Since demand conditions facing stage two, and cost conditions facing stage one are unchanged, this merely transfers profits from the first to the second stage, leaving profits of the combined firm the same as before vertical integration. Likewise, combined profits will not be increased if the second stage of the combined firm pays more to the first stage for inputs; this merely transfers profits from the second to the first stage.

In case 3, if the monopoly is at the second stage, formerly buying inputs from a purely competitive earlier stage, it is easy to understand why vertical integration between the two stages will not affect the price and output of the final product. Before integration, the supply curve of the purely competitive stage was part of the average cost curve of the monopolist; after vertical integration this is still the case, the only difference being that the portion of average cost formerly comprising the monopolist's purchases from other firms is now part of the value added of the integrated firm.

It is less obvious, but equally true, that vertical integration between a monopolist at stage one and a purely competitive industry at stage two will leave the level of final output unchanged (given constant final demand conditions and cost conditions at each stage of production). It is less obvious because, after all, elementary economic theory concludes that, all other things remaining equal, monopolization of a purely competitive industry will raise price and reduce output in that industry. However, this proposition concerning monopoly and the level of output is valid as long as there is a monopoly at *any one* of a number of separate successive stages in the productive process, and mere combination of successive stages will not change the level of output because the already existing monopoly at one stage will have *taken into account* the effect of its output level on the price of the final product. Figure 8–1 may help to clarify this point.

In order to simplify the diagrammatic exposition, it is assumed that one unit of the output of Stage 2 requires one unit of the output of Stage 1; that is, it is assumed that the inputs are combined in fixed proportions to yield a unit of the final product. This means that revenues and costs associated with levels of output of one stage can be expressed as a function of levels of output of the other stage also. Before integration, the demand curve confronting the monopolist at Stage 1 is a derived demand curve, obtained by subtracting from the demand price associated with any given quantity of the final product, the average cost (AC_2) of transforming a unit of the monopolist's product into a unit of the final product. The profit-maximizing monopolist will

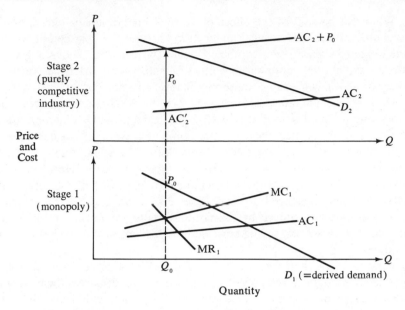

Figure 8-1 Vertical Integration between a Monopolist and a
Purely Competitive Industry

sell Q_0 units of output at P_0 per unit, and the total supply price of final
output will be $(AC'_2 + P_0)$.

In order to examine the effect of vertical integration on the level of
output, let us concentrate on the diagram depicting equilibrium at
Stage 1. When the two firms combine, the monopolist's demand curve
shifts upward and becomes the final demand curve; also, the monopolist's average cost curve shifts upward, because the average cost of
performing Stage 2 is now added to that of Stage 1 in order to obtain
the average cost of performing both stages in the integrated firm. What
effect will this have on the optimal (profit-maximizing) level of output?
The answer is none, for although the monopolist's marginal revenue and
marginal cost curves both change as the result of vertical integration,
they each change by the same amount at any given level of output.[1]

---

[1] Since, for any given quantity of output,

      final demand-price   =   derived demand-price   +   Stage 2 AC

and

      combined AC   =   Stage 1 AC   +   Stage 2 AC

it follows that the demand price and average cost associated with any given
level of the monopolist's output are each increased by the same amount as a
result of vertical integration. Hence TC and TR are each increased by the
same amount at any given level of output. Selecting any two levels of output,
and using subscripts to refer to these two levels of output,

What can be said of the effect of vertical integration on the optimal level of final output if vertical integration changes the cost conditions at one or more stages of the combined firm? By using the above analysis, we can explain the condition that must be satisfied in order that vertical integration *will not* change the optimal level of final output.

If, for example, vertical integration reduces the average cost of producing the final output, it is as though, in the previous diagram, after vertical integration has occurred, the combined average cost curve now shifts down. At any output level, this will reduce the total cost associated with the two stages of the productive process. However, the optimal level of output will not be changed if the slope of the total cost curve remains unchanged at every level of output. For this to happen, total cost must be reduced by the same absolute amount at any level of output, that is, the cost saving must be independent of the level of output produced.

It is apparent that, even apart from the case of price discrimination or that of bilateral monopoly, both of which are discussed below, one must qualify the statement that vertical integration will leave the optimal level of output of the final product unchanged. For this to be the case, either vertical integration must not change cost conditions at any stage of the productive process or, if it does so, any change in total cost must be independent of the level of output produced.

There are two cases in which vertical integration may change the output level and price of the final product, even though demand conditions for the final product, and cost conditions at each stage of the productive process, remain unchanged. The first is associated with price discrimination, the second with bilateral monopoly, which is a situation in which a single seller, or monopolist, deals with a single buyer, or monopsonist.

Forward vertical integration by a monopolist may permit a policy of price discrimination, formerly impossible because of the possibility of resale between different sectors of the monopolist's market, to be practiced. For reasons explained in Chapter 4, the ability to discriminate on a price basis may either increase or decrease the optimal level of the monopolist's output, and hence the output of the final product.

---

change in TR_2 − change in TR_1 = change in slope of TR

and

change in TC_2 − change in TC_1 = change in slope of TC

Since the change in TR_2 is equal to the change in TC_2, and since the change in TR_1 equals the change in TC_1, the slope of the TR curve is changed by the same amount as the slope of the TC curve; that is, marginal revenue and marginal cost are changed by the same amount at any level of output.

Finally, still assuming constant demand conditions for the final product and unchanged cost conditions at each stage, vertical integration between a monopolist and a monopsonist at successive stages of the productive process can, in certain circumstances, lower the price and increase output of the final product. This can be illustrated with the aid of Figure 8–2.

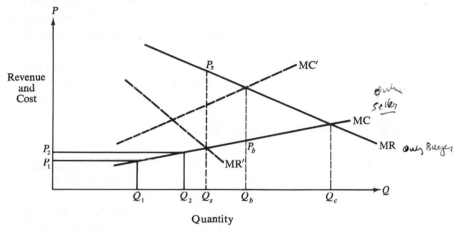

Figure 8–2   Vertical Integration and Bilateral Monopoly

The curve labeled MC is the marginal cost curve of S, the monopolist, and MR is the marginal revenue product curve of B, the monopsonist. Curve MR indicates the marginal revenue obtained by B from employing different quantities of the monopolist's output. At a fixed price, such as P_1, S would be willing to supply Q_1 units of output (an amount which equates the monopolist's marginal revenue and marginal cost), at P_2, S would be willing to supply Q_2, and so on. That is, the average cost curve of the product to the buyer, B, is MC, and the curve marginal to MC, labeled MC' in Figure 8–2, is the marginal cost of the product to B. The monopsonist would maximize profits if price were P_b and quantity supplied Q_b, for at this combination B's marginal cost (MC') equals his marginal revenue product (MR). The monopolist, S, however, desires a different price-quantity combination. MR indicates the quantities that B would be willing to buy at alternative fixed prices of the monopolist's product, and is therefore the average revenue curve of the monopolist. The curve marginal to MR, labeled MR', is therefore the marginal revenue to S, and the monopolist would maximize profits if price were P_s and quantity demanded Q_s.

The price agreed, and quantity of the monopolist's product traded, will depend upon bargaining between the parties, and there are numerous possibilities. If bargaining takes place in terms of price only, the agreed price will lie between P_s and P_b because, at a price above P_s both parties would agree to lower price, while at a price below P_b both parties would agree to raise price. The output traded at the agreed price may, however, be less than Q_c, the output level which maximizes the joint profits of the two firms. If the two firms integrate, the output decision will be determined with regard to the original MR and MC curves, and the level of output of the intermediate product may be increased relative to the output resulting under bilateral monopoly. Given the assumption of fixed production coefficients between the output of the monopolist and the final product sold by the monopsonist, levels of intermediate output indicate also quantities of the final product.

Vertical Integration and Entry Barriers

The previous section considered how vertical integration affects the pricing behavior of established firms in an industry, given the demand conditions for the final product facing the industry group. The question considered in this section is whether, and if so how, does vertical integration affect the behavior of potential entrants. In this context the relevant question to be answered is the following. Does vertical integration by established firms affect either the potential entrant's cost or demand conditions? For, as explained in Chapter 7, it is these two sets of conditions that determine whether a potential entrant will enter an industry.

The relationship between vertical integration and entry barriers is a matter about which there is still a certain amount of controversy, even among economists. All that can be done in a book of this nature is to point out the nature of arguments linking vertical integration to entry barriers.

One must compare the situation in which a potential entrant at some stage (Stage 2) in the process of production and distribution is confronted by established firms performing only that stage, with a situation in which the established firms performing that stage also perform earlier (Stage 1), or later (Stage 3), stages.

Let us assume for the moment that vertical integration has no effect upon cost conditions at any stage of production. The potential entrant may face increased entry barriers for either of the two following reasons. First, backward vertical integration by established firms at Stage 2 may enable the latter to acquire control of scarce raw materials required by a Stage 2 entrant and hence deter entry at Stage 2 by simply refusing to supply inputs to a new entrant. In these circumstances, the entry restrictions on Stage 2 are founded upon entry restrictions at Stage 1, and the returns earned at Stage 1 by vertically integrated firms will consist primarily of the rents associated with a scarce resource. Nonetheless, by deterring entry at Stage 2, control of Stage 1 may enable the integrated firms to earn higher returns at Stage 2 than they would have earned in the absence of integration. Although, in the absence of integration, entry at Stage 1 is still effectively barred, the independent Stage 1 firms may supply new entrants and established firms at Stage 2 alike; the new entrant at Stage 2 can compete for inputs with established firms at Stage 2, in contrast to the situation in which established firms at Stage 2 also control Stage 1. Forward vertical integration by established firms at Stage 2 may increase barriers to entry for similar reasons, if it confers upon established firms a monopoly over limited distributive outlets at Stage 3. Such outlets may be limited in number for legal reasons such as licensing requirements or zoning laws. In the absence of control of Stage 3 by established firms, demand for the product of an entrant at Stage 2 depends upon the entrant's anticipations regarding the post-entry price and/or output policies of established firms at Stage 2. If established firms control Stage 3, and refuse to buy from the entrant, entry will be unprofitable irrespective of established firms' Stage 2 behavior.

Second, even though established integrated firms do not have complete control over limited inputs required at Stage 2, or of limited distributive outlets at Stage 3, a refusal by established firms to supply, or purchase from, an unintegrated entrant at Stage 2 may mean that the new entrant is compelled to begin operations at both stages. This will increase the amount of capital required for entry, compared to single-stage entry. Increased capital requirements may increase barriers to entry if there is a constraint on capital funds facing the potential entrant. This last point is important, for unless the potential entrant is unable to obtain the required amount of capital, or must pay more than established integrated firms for capital, increased capital requirements themselves do not increase barriers to entry. Since potential entrants may be large firms established in other industries, rather than newly created firms, there is no a priori reason why potential entrants should have less access to internally generated, or external, funds in amounts and at terms which are similar to those applying in the case of established firms.

If vertical integration lowers cost, single-stage entry by a new entrant will mean that the entrant's costs are higher, relative to the costs of established firms at that stage, than if established firms were unintegrated. However, any cost reduction occasioned by vertical integration is not, itself, an increased barrier to entry. The entrant can achieve the same cost savings by entering as a vertically integrated unit, and only if there is a constraint on the entrant's capital funds will this be impossible. Given such a constraint, vertical integration by established firms which makes it necessary for the entrant to enter more than one stage in order to be just as efficient as established firms will make entry more difficult. However, if vertical integration lowers costs, it is desirable on grounds of efficiency that entrants should be forced to integrate.

Measurement of Vertical Integration

Hypotheses regarding the relationship between vertical integration and other characteristics of industrial structure must be tested with respect to their factual relevance. This requires a quantifiable measure of the degree of vertical integration. Several different methods of measuring the degree of vertical integration, in the sense of the number of vertically related stages performed by a firm operating in a particular industry, have been discussed in the literature dealing with industrial structure.

One possible index employs the ratio of value added (that is, sales less expenditures for raw materials, fuel, and power) by a firm to the firm's sales revenues. The rationale underlying the use of such a measure is that the more successive stages in the productive process that are performed by a firm, the greater will be the magnitude of this ratio. Such a measure has, however, several defects as an index of the degree of vertical integration.

Differences in the rate of change over time of input and output prices respectively will change the index even though the physical processes performed by a firm remain unchanged. As a result, the reliability of the index as an indicator of changes in the degree of vertical integration over time may be impaired.

Value added includes profits and, comparing two firms performing identical productive operations, the firm with greater profits will show a higher index of integration. Hence the index is not a reliable measure of vertical integration even with respect to firms operating at the same stage in the same industry.

If one attempts to use the index to compare the degree of vertical integration in different firms, whether in the same or in different industries, even greater limitations reveal themselves. Suppose that each of the successive stages involved in the production of a particular final product is performed by a separate firm, and that each firm contributes an equal amount to the total value of the final product. The degree of vertical integration, measured by the ratio of value added to sales, will decline progressively as one considers firms closer to the final stage, despite the fact that all firms are by definition equally integrated. Since the index reflects the stage in the productive process which is being measured, rather than the degree of vertical integration, the index is of little use even when comparing different firms in the same industry unless they are at the same stage in the productive process. When making comparisions between firms in different industries, the index will yield even more ambiguous results.

Another defect of the index, closely related to the last, arises when using the index to indicate changes in vertical integration. The index will reflect differences in the direction of vertical integration, yielding different values for the same increase in value added, depending upon whether the additional stages previously preceded or succeeded the firm's original operations. Thus, if two firms, originally located at the same stage in the same industry integrate in opposite directions, each firm taking over one additional stage which contributes an equal amount to the value of the final product, the index will show a greater degree of vertical integration for the firm integrating backward than for the firm integrating forward. Similarly, forward integration by a raw material producer yields no change in the index—it remains unchanged at a value of unity.

The ratio of the value of inventory to sales has been suggested as an alternative measure of the degree of vertical integration. The notion that increases in this index indicate a larger number of successive stages performed by the firm rests upon the implicit assumption that the greater the number of stages performed, the greater will be the level of the firm's total inventory. Vertical integration which enables a firm to economize on stocks will invalidate this line of reasoning and result in a smaller value of the index the larger the number of stages performed. Like the ratio of value added to sales, the ratio of inventory to sales will be affected by differential rates of change in inventory and final product prices respectively. Such changes will change the index even though the number of stages, and physical characteristics of the firm's operations, remain unchanged.

The ratio of value added to sales and the ratio of inventory to sales both attempt to measure the degree of vertical integration in the sense of the number of successive stages performed by a firm selling in a particular market. A slightly different kind of index of vertical integration shows the degree to which a firm performing any particular stage of production or distribution is dependent upon markets for obtaining the inputs of that stage, or for the disposal of the output of that stage. This requires separate measures of the degree of backward and forward integration for each stage of production or distribution performed by a firm. For example, total interfirm purchases, or transfers, of inputs required at a particular stage, expressed as a proportion of the total amount of the input used by the firm, yields a measure of backward vertical integration at that stage. This measure indicates the extent to which the firm relies upon the market to supply it with inputs at any particular stage of the productive process. Similarly, total inter-firm transfers of the output of a particular stage, expressed as a proportion of the total output of that stage, measures the degree of forward vertical integration at that stage and indicates the extent to which the firm performing that stage is dependent upon the market for disposition of its product.

An advantage of this type of measure is that either value or quantity data may be employed and the ratios are invariant to price level changes since both numerator and denominator of the value ratios involve use of the same price. Most of the problems arising out of the use of such measures are likely to revolve around the definition of a stage in the productive process. Much of industry involves two or more successive stages in production which might theoretically be split among two or more producers. However, attention is generally focused upon those situations in which successive stages of production controlled by a single managerial supervision are also, or were previously, performed by separate firms.

RECOMMENDED READINGS

1. Adelman, M. A., "Concept and Statistical Measurement of Vertical Integration," in G. J. Stigler (ed.), *Business Concentration and Price Policy* (Princeton, N. J.: Princeton University Press, 1955).
2. ———, "Integration and the Antitrust Laws," *Harvard Law Review*, 1949.
3. Bork, R., "Vertical Integration and the Sherman Act: The Legal History of an Economic Misconception," *University of Chicago Law Review*, Autumn 1954, pp. 194–201.
4. ———, W. S. Bowman, H. M. Blake, and W. K. Jones, "The Goals of Antitrust: A Dialogue on Policy," *Columbia Law Review*, March 1965, pp. 363–466, especially pp. 389–394, 403–412, 417–422, 440–458, 463–466.
5. Coase, R. H., "The Nature of the Firm," *Economica*, November 1937; reprinted in R. B. Heflebower and G. W. Stocking (eds.) *Readings in Price Theory* (Homewood, Ill.: Richard D. Irwin, Inc.; 1952). Published under the sponsorship of the American Economic Association.
6. Comanor, W. S., "Vertical Mergers, Market Powers, and the Antitrust Laws," *American Economic Review*, Papers and Proceedings, May 1967, pp. 254–65 (with comment by J. S. McGee, *American Economic Review*, pp. 269–70).
7. Machlup, F., and M. Taber, Bilateral Monopoly, Successive Monopoly, and Vertical Integration," *Economica*, May 1960.

CHAPTER NINE

DIVERSIFICATION

Motives for Diversification

Diversification refers to the extent to which a firm produces a variety of different kinds of output. As usual, the definition of what constitutes a different product is crucial in determining the degree of diversification existing at any particular point in time. Vertical integration, strictly speaking, is an aspect of diversification. However, the motives associated with diversification and vertical integration are somewhat different, and the term diversification will be used to refer to production of different products which are not vertically related to each other.

Diversification, like other features of industrial structure, is the result of firms' attempts to achieve certain objectives, such as profit, sales revenue, or growth rate maximization. Whatever objective is being pursued, it is useful to distinguish two major motives for diversification, one associated with risk and uncertainty, and one associated with factors operating even in the absence of uncertainty.

Even in the absence of uncertainty, a firm will compare the extent to which diversification, as opposed to expansion of its existing activities, will best achieve the firm's objectives. A firm can be expected to diversify, rather than grow within the scope of its existing product structure, if the former alternative promises a higher prospective rate of return.

The influence of uncertainty upon decision making has already been referred to in Chapter 1. In conditions of uncertainty, the revenues anticipated by the decision maker as a result of investment of a given amount of money capital in productive activities will take the form of a range of possible outcomes, each associated with a probability assigned by the decision maker. Considering the profit probability distribution associated with producing a single product, part of the uncertainty is due to the possibility of buyers spending their incomes in other markets. If the firm also operates in these markets, the variability of expected earnings will be reduced. The probability of an extreme occurrence, such as loss in all markets, is less than the probability of loss in any single market. A firm may therefore invest its capital resources in diversified activities, even though the mean probable expected sales revenue and earnings from investing in a single activity are the same, in order to reduce the risk associated with its capital investment. In this connection risk is defined as the variance of possible outcomes associated with the investment of a given sum in productive activities.

The problem of reducing random variations in sales and earnings must not be confused with the problem of cyclical instability arising from changes in the level of activity in the economy as a whole. Cyclical, as opposed to random, sources of instability lend themselves to prediction. A mere increase in the number of activities without reference to cyclical patterns need not reduce cyclical instability. Moreover, there is no a priori reason why diversification should necessarily produce more cyclical stability than specialization. Specializing in a cyclically stable industry may achieve this as effectively as diversifying into a number of industries which differ in cyclical stability, but which vary in opposite ways so that demand for the products of the group as a whole remains constant at any stage of the cycle.

Diversification and Other Structural Features

The degree of diversification in a firm will be influenced by cost conditions associated with individual products. If economies of scale exist in the production of individual products, a firm will have to produce a certain minimum scale of output of any individual product in order to be able to compete effectively with larger firms. Given a limitation on the amount of investment funds available to the firm, this will place a limit upon the degree of diversification possible. In other words, economies of scale may explain why the profitability of diversification is lower than that of specialization at small firm sizes.

Empirical evidence obtained in a study of diversification in the United States by M. Gort[1] indicates that the degree of diversification, measured in terms of the number of industries in which a firm operates, increases as firm size increases. To some extent, this may reflect the

---

[1] See reference (2) at the end of this chapter.

existence of economies of scale, as already mentioned. However, it may also reflect the fact that further expansion in existing markets is expected to be less profitable than diversification. Whether a firm will diversify or grow in other directions will be influenced by the relative profitability of these alternative methods of growth. The profitability of expansion in existing markets will be influenced by the rate at which the total market demand is expected to increase. Other things being equal, one might therefore expect diversification and the rate of increase of demand in the firm's original, or primary, industry to be inversely related; in fact, Gort's empirical evidence suggests that diversification and the rate of increase of demand in a firm's primary industry are positively related. A possible explanation is that expansion through diversification requires funds, and faster growth in primary industries will generate more funds to finance expansion.

Apart from the expected rate of growth of market demand, the profitability of expansion in existing markets will also be influenced by factors limiting the growth of market shares of individual firms. One would expect it to be more difficult, other things being equal, for firms to grow profitably in original markets in which sellers are large and few in number. In these circumstances, efforts to obtain a larger share of a stable total market are more likely to be noticed and countered by sellers in the market. This expectation seems to be borne out by the statistical evidence obtained by Gort, which shows that diversification and concentration in primary industries are positively associated.

We turn now from factors influencing the profitability of expansion in existing markets to those influencing the profitability of diversification. Although empirical evidence revealed by Gort's study shows that diversification and concentration in a firm's original markets are positively related, high concentration in receiving industries does not seem to have deterred diversification. In many cases, diversification has involved entry into highly concentrated industries.

Diversification is, however, associated with technological change and high industry growth rates in the receiving industries, both of which indicate relatively low barriers to entry into the industries concerned. Rapid growth of market demand makes it easier for a firm to enter an industry without encroaching upon the markets of established firms in the industry, and therefore reduces barriers to entry into such industries. Given the reaction of established firms anticipated by potential entrants, the expected profitability of entering such industries will be greater than the profitability of entry into industries with stable market demand. The available evidence suggests that the rate of technological change is even more important than growth of market demand in influencing a firm's choice of industry as a diversification outlet, for it shows that firms have diversified largely into industries characterized by rapid technological change, measured by high increases in labor productivity, and ratios of technical to other personnel. Due to changing technologies, new firms may in fact have a cost advantage over established firms in the industry.

In addition to being an alternative to expansion in existing markets, diversification is also an alternative to growth through vertical integration. Gort's study indicates that diversification and vertical integration are inversely related. Even if diversification is less profitable than vertical integration, a firm may diversify in order to reduce risk. Vertical integration, like horizontal expansion in existing markets, cannot reduce risk, in the sense of the variability of a firm's earnings. This is because the demand for goods and services at each of several successive stages of production depends ultimately upon the demand for the final product, and will vary in the same direction in response to variations in the latter. Thus vertical integration cannot reduce the instability of a firm's earnings by generating offsetting increases in sales at one stage of the productive process for random and cyclical contractions in demand at another stage.

The study by Gort indicates that diversification and firm growth rates are not closely related. This is hardly surprising, for although diversification is a form of growth, firms may also diversify their activities and replace existing activities by new ones in response to a decline in profitability of the former, even though the total level of the firm's operations remains unchanged. Furthermore, in those situations in which firms grow, there is no a priori reason why growth through diversification should in all circumstances be considered more profitable or achieve other objectives better than growth through expansion in existing markets or vertical integration. That is, there is no a priori reason why firms which grow by diversification should grow more than firms which grow in other directions. The relationship between diversification and growth is a consequence of reciprocal influences, some of them leading to a positive, some to a negative association between these two variables. The direction of causation in the relationship between diversification and firm growth is by no means clear. On the one hand, diversification is a form of growth, on the other hand firms growing faster may earn higher rates of return and thus generate a larger volume of investment funds from earnings—funds which may be used to diversify.

Gort's statistical evidence likewise reveals little systematic relationship between diversification and profits. Again, reciprocal influences are at work. One might expect high profits and diversification to be related either because profits are a source of investment funds which can be used to finance diversification or because diversification increases profits.

Firms may, however, use their funds to expand in a horizontal or vertical direction. Similarly, the absence of a systematic relationship between profits and diversification does not imply that diversification fails to increase profits; it may merely reflect the fact that for some firms, the anticipated profits from growing in other ways are greater. Also, where a firm diversifies for defensive reasons, the firm's profits may even decline on balance; they may, however, have declined less than in the absence of diversification.

Diversification and Competition

Diversification may be important in providing increased competition. In this context it is necessary to distinguish diversification accomplished by acquisition and/or merger between the diversifying firm and a firm already operating in another industry, and that achieved by entry in the sense of a new firm with new capacity operating in the industry. To the extent that diversification increases the number of firms operating in a given industry, this may increase competition in the industry. Many instances of diversification covered by the Gort study involved entry into highly concentrated industries, and in a significant proportion of these industries, the entering firm became a leading producer. One must not, however, jump to the conclusion that diversification which occurs through acquisition and merger, and which does not change the number of firms operating in a given industry, will leave the pattern of behavior in the industry unchanged. Gort's evidence, for example, shows that many instances of diversification have been accomplished through merger, and that mergers frequently initiate further subsequent expansion in the newly entered industry, that is, a change in behavior of the acquired firm compared to its behavior prior to the merger. Thus, it is not essential that diversification should occur through new entry in order that competition be affected.

In addition to the relationship between diversification and competition in general, that between diversification and R&D competition in particular has attracted a considerable amount of attention from economists. One hypothesis that has been advanced is that diversification stimulates invention. The argument, in brief, is that research yields inventions and discoveries in unexpected areas. A diversified firm, it is argued, will generally be able to produce and market a higher proportion of these unexpected inventions than a firm whose product line is narrow. Therefore, it is argued, the expected profitability of research is greater for highly diversified firms, and such firms will tend to support more research than less diversified firms.

This argument implies that new knowledge is worth more to firms which use the knowledge themselves rather than license or sell the knowledge to other firms. Why should the expected profitability of an invention which is patented by a firm and leased or sold to other firms for commercial exploitation be less than the expected profitability of the same invention assuming that the firm uses the invention itself? One possible explanation might be that the market for ideas is imperfect and that the firm will receive less by selling the invention than it can earn by exploiting the invention itself because other firms are imperfectly informed of the existence or potential applications of the invention when offered for sale.

Empirical evidence obtained by Gort and others[2] shows that diversification and R&D are indeed closely related. Diversification, measured by the number of industries in which a firm operates, is strongly correlated in a positive manner with R&D inputs, measured by R&D expenditures, scientific manpower, and the ratio of technical to other personnel, and also with R&D output, measured by patents issued. At first sight, the evidence seems consistent with the hypothesis that diversification increases invention. On further inspection, however, it can be argued[3] that the relationship is largely spurious. Little relationship between R&D input, or output, remains after allowing for the influence of technological opportunities upon the observed relationship. That is, technological opportunity is generally greater in those industries into which firms diversify than in the original industry of the firm. After diversification, a larger proportion of the firm's operations takes place in industries in which the ratio of R&D input to other inputs is high relative to the ratio in a firm's original industry. Accordingly, higher degrees of diversification and a larger ratio of R&D to other inputs go hand in hand, considering the firm's total operations. The influence of technological opportunity upon the observed relationship between diversification and R&D can be eliminated by comparing more diversified and less diversified firms operating in industries which individually have roughly similar ratios of R&D input to total input. If more diversified firms tended to do more R&D in these circumstances, the evidence would be more consistent with the hypothesis that diversification per se increases invention. As yet, however, there is little evidence in support of this contention, while some evidence tends to reject the hypothesis. For example, evidence relating to the pharmaceutical industry in the United States[4] showed that innovation (mea-

[2] See L. R. Amey, reference (1), and F. M. Scherer, reference (3), for example.
[3] See F. M. Scherer, reference (3).
[4] See W. S. Comanor "Research & Technical Change in the Pharmaceutical Industry," *Review of Economics & Statistics*, May 1965, p. 184.

sured by the value of two years sales of new products) was inversely related to the extent of diversification within the pharmaceutical industry. That is, measuring diversification by the division of output among various pharmaceutical product submarkets, the statistical evidence suggests that for a given level of R&D input, higher rates of technical change will be achieved if a firm's product line is narrow rather than broad.

Measures of Diversification

The degree of diversification within a firm, or industry, will be directly dependent upon the way in which different products are defined. The narrower the industrial classification employed, the greater will be the observed degree of diversification in firms, or industries.

An index of diversification which has been employed in some statistical studies consists of the ratio of a firm's nonprimary output, or employment, to the total output, or employment, of the firm. The primary output may be defined with respect to the SIC industry into which a firm is classified. A limitation of such a measure is illustrated by comparing two firms, each of which shows an identical ratio of nonprimary to total output, but the nonprimary output of one firm is divided between a number of industries whereas in the other firm it is concentrated in a single industry. No difference in diversification would be revealed, though for most purposes the first firm may be considered to be more diversified.

Another way to measure the degree of diversification is simply to count the number of industries in which a firm produces goods or services. Such a measure has also been employed in empirical studies. Some economists have argued that such a measure gives undue weight to many activities which, in the aggregate, account for only a small proportion of a firm's total operations. For example, a simple count suggests that a firm with fewer products than another, but with larger absolute levels of output of each product, is less diversified. According to this line of reasoning, one should have some idea of the size of a firm's operations in each industry and take this into account in calculating an index of diversification.

Composite measures of diversification, which attempt to combine the two types of measure already mentioned, have also been employed in statistical studies. One such index is obtained by multiplying the ratio of nonprimary to total output, or employment, by the number of industries in which the firm operates. Another alternative is to count the number of industries that account for a specified percentage of the total output or employment of the firm. The larger the resulting number, the more diversified the firm. The great danger in using such composite indices is that they conceal more information than they reveal. For example, if the ratio of nonprimary to total output in one firm is 1 to 2, and the firm operates in five other industries in addition to the primary industry, the first composite index mentioned yields 6/2, = 3, which would also result in the case of a firm operating in 12 industries, with a ratio of non primary to total output of 1 to 4. Clearly, no *single* index can indicate what are essentially differences in two or more dimensions of firm size. The least ambiguous approach is perhaps a simple count of industries, accompanied, if considered necessary, by a separate index of absolute size in each industry, such as employment or sales.

Any measure of diversification which employs size variables such as employment, assets, or net output, may reflect aspects of firm size other than diversification. The use of employment or assets as a size variable involves problems of allocating nonspecific inputs between different products, a more or less arbitrary procedure in some firms. In addition, all three size variables will reflect vertical aspects of firm size in addition to diversification. If, for example, two firms are identical in all respects except that one firm is more vertically integrated than another in producing one of its final products, employment, asset, or net output weights will assign a greater degree of diversification to that firm. The resulting index will reflect vertical diversification in addition to diversification proper. For these reasons, sales might be a more appropriate size variable with which to measure diversification. Of course, even a simple count of industries in which a firm operates will reflect vertical integration unless industries that are vertically related are counted only once.

Whatever the measure considered appropriate, the degree of diversification within establishments controlled by a firm cannot generally be ascertained from official statistics. In census of production and other data, the output or employment of establishments producing more than one product as defined by the official product classification is generally classified under the heading of the principal product of the establishment. For this reason, precise calculation of diversification from official statistics is impossible, even if one accepts the official classification of products as appropriate.

As usual, a priori reasoning alone cannot provide a complete answer to the question of which measure of diversification is the most appropriate. Empirical investigation of which measure of diversification is closely related to other aspects of firm behavior may provide a guide to the best measure, in the sense of the measure with most predictive value. Close relationship itself, however, does not necessarily imply cause and effect.

RECOMMENDED READINGS

1. Amey, L. R., "Diversified Manufacturing Businesses," *Journal of the Royal Statistical Society*, Series A, Vol. 127, Part 2, 1964.
2. Gort, M., *Diversification and Integration in American Industry* (Princeton, N. J.: Princeton University Press, 1962).
3. Scherer, F. M., "Firm Size, Market Structure, Opportunity, and the Output of Patented Inventions," *American Economic Review*, December 1965, especially pp. 1114–1116.

CHAPTER TEN

PUBLIC POLICY AND INDUSTRIAL STRUCTURE

Public Policy Objectives

If public policy towards industry is to amount to more than the whim of politicians or bureaucrats, laws against price agreements, horizontal and vertical mergers, or any other interference with the unregulated pattern of industrial structure must be shown to contribute towards some generally accepted objective or objectives. Which structure of industry is desirable depends upon the nature of the objectives being pursued. Some objectives may have little to do with economics; a number of commentators on the United States antitrust laws are of the opinion, for example, that these laws have been more concerned with preserving small firms on the grounds of protecting democratic institutions, securing equality of opportunity, improving business ethics, and discouraging behavior which offends notions of fair play than with securing good economic performance. The pursuit of some objectives may even conflict with the achievement of economic objectives; one might, for example, favor an industrial structure involving small individual proprietorships, despite the fact that economic efficiency in some sense is thereby impaired, if one believes that such a structure is desirable on the grounds of securing equality of opportunity, or preserving democratic institutions, or on other social grounds. The economist has no special competence for choosing what the objectives of public policy shall be. Nonetheless, it may still be important to know the cost, in terms of the alternative economic benefits foregone, of achieving noneconomic objectives.

This chapter deals solely with possible economic objectives underlying public policy towards industrial structure, and with the measures designed to achieve these objectives. One objective which has long occupied a central place in economic theory, and which is sometimes claimed to be the basis of much existing public policy towards business, is that of maximizing the welfare derived by the community from the use of its scarce productive resources. The welfare of the community is said to depend upon the level of subjective satisfaction experienced by each of its individual members, and this in turn will be influenced by three aspects of economic performance, namely, how the community's resources are allocated between different kinds of output, what methods are used to produce the output, and how the output is allocated among members of the community.

The productive resources of the community, consisting of human skills, the stock of fixed capital equipment, and natural resources, are capable of producing many different alternative combinations of output. One aspect of economic performance, which we shall refer to as allocative efficiency, is the extent to which the existing combination of outputs corresponds to the combination which will maximize the aggregate welfare of individual members of the community. Another question is whether resources producing any particular output combination are allocated in such a manner that the output in question is being produced efficiently. We shall refer to this aspect of economic performance as technical efficiency. Finally, irrespective of what is produced or how efficiently it is produced, there is the question of how any particular aggregate output should be allocated among members of the community in order to maximize welfare. We shall refer to this aspect of economic performance as distributive efficiency.

The welfare of the community cannot be said to be maximized if it is possible, by changing the existing resource allocation or distribution of output among members of the community, to increase the satisfaction of some members without reducing the satisfaction of any other members. A situation in which all possible improvements of this variety have been made is referred to as a Pareto optimum, after the economist Vilfredo Pareto who originally formulated the criterion. Although distributive, technical, and allocative efficiency are related, we shall in the remainder of this section consider them separately in turn. In each case, certain conditions are outlined which must be fulfilled in order that the welfare of the community be maximized according to the Pareto criterion. In addition, the manner in which the welfare of the community can be improved by a change in resource allocation or output distribution if these conditions are violated is explained.

Consider first, the characteristics of an optimal distribution of products among consumers. In order that a particular aggregate output of products be distributed optimally among members of the community, it must be impossible, by reallocating the output among consumers, to make someone better off without making someone else worse off. This requires that the ratio of the marginal utilities of any two products be the same for all consumers. Marginal utility refers to the change in satisfaction experienced by an individual consumer as the result of increasing or reducing by one unit the quantity of a particular commodity consumed. Marginal utility itself is subjective and cannot be measured; however, a ratio of marginal utilities—termed a marginal rate of substitution (hereafter referred to as MRS) expresses an individual consumer's relative evaluation of one additional unit of one good in terms of another good, and can be measured. Symbolically, the condition for an optimal allocation of output among consumers can be written as

$$\frac{MU_x^1}{MU_y^1} = \frac{MU_x^2}{MU_y^2} = \frac{MU_x^3}{MU_y^3} = \cdots$$

where the subscripts x and y refer to two different products and the superscripts 1, 2, 3 $\cdots$ refer to different individuals. Hereafter this condition, that the MRS between any two goods shall be the same for all consumers, is referred to as rule one. This is the rule of distributive efficiency.

As the reader can easily verify for himself, if the condition were violated so that an additional unit of good X were not worth the same number of units of good Y to two different consumers, both consumers can increase the total satisfaction they derive from consumption by exchanging some of the goods which they possess. If, for example, given the combination of apples and bananas which consumer A possesses, he values an extra apple at one banana (that is, the marginal utility of an apple, and that of a banana, are the same for A) and consumer B values an extra banana at two apples (that is, the marginal utility of a banana is twice the marginal utility of an apple for B) both can experience an increase in total satisfaction by exchanging goods, B giving A anything between one and two apples in exchange for one banana. The possibility of mutually advantageous exchange will continue to exist until the ratio of marginal utilities associated with apples and bananas is the same for both A and B.

Next we turn to the problem of technical efficiency in producing a given combination of products. In order that a given combination of products be produced as efficiently as possible, it must be impossible to produce the same combination of products by using fewer productive resources, or inputs. This requires that the ratio of marginal physical products of any two inputs be the same in the production of all different commodities produced. The marginal physical product of an input refers to the change in total output of a product when the amount of the input in question is increased or decreased by one unit. Symbolically, the condition for efficient allocation of inputs between the production of different outputs can be stated as follows:

$$\frac{MPP_x^i}{MPP_x^j} = \frac{MPP_y^i}{MPP_y^j} = \frac{MPP_z^i}{MPP_z^j} = \ldots$$

where the superscripts i and j are inputs and the subscripts $x, y, z \ldots$ refer to different products. This condition will hereafter be referred to as rule two, and is the rule of technical efficiency.

The reader can verify for himself, by substituting numbers into the ratios, that if the ratios differ, it is possible to produce the same total output while using fewer resources. Suppose, for example, that the relevant numbers are:

$$\frac{MPP_x^{labor}}{MPP_x^{capital}} = \frac{4}{10} \quad \text{and} \quad \frac{MPP_y^{labor}}{MPP_y^{capital}} = \frac{}{6}$$

By transferring one unit of capital input from the production of Y (which tends to reduce total output of Y by 6 units) into production of X (which tends to increase output of X by 10 units), and substituting one and a half units of labor input from X into Y production in order to leave the total output of Y unchanged, the effect is to increase output of X by 10 minus 6 equals 4 units. By implication, this demonstrates that the existing level of total output of X and Y, whatever its magnitude, can be produced with fewer resources. Efficiency in production is not optimal.

After considering the problem of efficiency in the production of any particular combination of products, we turn finally to the problem of securing an optimal allocation of resources between different alternative combinations of products, the problem of allocative efficiency. Given any particular combination of outputs which is being produced, the rate at which one good, say X, can be transformed into another good, say Y, by shifting resources from X production into Y production is called the marginal rate of transformation (MRT). If rule one is satisfied, the combination of outputs will be distributed among members of the community in such a manner that the rate at which any consumer is willing to exchange X for Y (the marginal rate of substitution) is the same for all consumers. Unless, given the existing combination of products being produced, the rate at which every member of the community would be willing to exchange one good for the other (given by the MRS) is equal to the rate at which that good can be transformed into the other by reallocating resources between the products (given by the MRT), it would be possible to make some members of the community better off and no one worse off by reallocating resources and producing more of one good and less of the other. Suppose, for example, that it is possible to obtain two X by diverting resources and reducing Y output by one unit, while the (equalized) MRS between X and Y is one, indicating that consumers would be willing to exchange one Y for one X. In these circumstances, by shifting resources and producing two more X and one less Y, and giving one additional X to people who have suffered a reduction in Y consumption, everyone would by definition be as well off as before; since we are then still left with one extra unit of X, which can be distributed among some or all members of the community, the satisfaction of some or all members of the community can be increased without reducing that of any other members.

The rule of optimal resource allocation dealing with allocative efficiency, hereafter referred to as rule three, is therefore that for any pair of commodities produced and consumed:

$$\text{MRS}_1 = \text{MRS}_2 = \text{MRS}_3 \ldots = \text{MRT}$$

where the subscripts denote different individuals and MRS, as already explained, is the ratio of the marginal utilities of the two commodities for the individual consumer to which the subscript refers. Unless this rule is satisfied, the allocation of resources between different kinds of output will not be optimal, for by shifting resources from the production of one good into the production of another good, it is possible to make some members of the community better off without making others worse off. We shall return to examine rule three in more detail after considering the way in which purely competitive pricing behavior satisfies the necessary conditions for economic efficiency discussed in this section.

Pure Competition and Resource Allocation

The properties of a purely competitive general equilibrium are alleged to result in an optimal allocation of resources among different kinds of output, an optimal manner of production of the output, and an optimal distribution of output among members of the community according to the Pareto criterion.

The requirements of rule one are satisfied for the following reasons. In order to maximize satisfaction, any individual must allocate his income between different goods in such a manner that the marginal utility of every good consumed is proportional to the price of the good; unless marginal utility is proportional to price, it follows that the individual can increase the total satisfaction which he derives from his income by reallocating his income and buying a different combination of goods. Each consumer, if he behaves optimally, will therefore buy commodities in such amounts that for him the ratio of marginal utilities of any pair of goods is equal to the price ratio of those goods. Since in pure competition the price of any good is the same for all consumers, and individual consumers cannot influence price, the ratio of marginal utilities of any pair of goods will be the same for all consumers. This will be so despite differences in tastes or incomes, which may result in different amounts of the goods purchased, comparing different consumers. Hence the requirements of rule one, the condition necessary for an optimal distribution of goods among consumers, will be satisfied.

The requirements of rule two are satisfied for the following reasons. Profit-maximizing producers will choose that combination of inputs which minimizes the total money cost of producing any given level of output they produce. For such a combination the ratio of the marginal physical productivities of any pair of inputs employed must be equal to the price ratio of the inputs; any input combination which does not satisfy this requirement will be inefficient in the sense that the same output can be produced at a lower money cost by using a different combination of inputs. Because, in pure competition, the price of any particular input is the same for all producers, producers of different products will employ combinations of inputs with identical marginal physical productivity ratios. Hence the requirements of rule two are satisfied—output will be produced efficiently.

The requirements of rule three are satisfied because, in pure competition, individual firms will produce a level of output which equates the marginal cost of producing a particular product with the price of the product. That is, for any pair of products, the ratio of the marginal costs of the products will equal the ratio of product prices. In pure competition the ratio of marginal costs is the marginal rate of transformation (MRT) between the two goods in question. For example, assuming, for expositional convenience only, that labor is the only input which can be reallocated between different industries, the marginal cost of any product equals the wage of labor divided by the marginal physical productivity (MPP) of labor in the production of that product. The marginal cost ratio of two products X and Y is therefore the ratio of the MPP of labor in Y production to the MPP of labor in X production. This is the rate at which X can be transformed into Y by shifting resources from X production into Y production. From rule one, consumers will all equate the marginal rate of substitution (MRS) between two goods with the price ratio of those two goods. If the MRS between two goods equals the price ratio of those goods, and the ratio of their marginal costs (equals MRT) equals the price ratio of the goods, it follows that MRS equals MRT. That is, the rate at which every consumer is willing to exchange one good for the other is equal to the rate at which the products can be transformed into each other by shifting resources; therefore it is impossible, by shifting resources between products, to make anyone better off without making someone else worse off.

The preceding paragraphs demonstrate that the requirements of an optimal resource allocation mentioned in the first section of this chapter will be met by a purely competitive general equilibrium. It is necessary to add that the analysis ignores second-order conditions; that is, an allocation may satisfy the three rules of the section entitled Public Policy Objectives and yet not be optimal unless certain additional conditions, referred to as second-order conditions, are also satisfied. The three rules are necessary, but not sufficient, for maximizing the aggregate welfare of individuals in the community according to the Pareto criterion.

Apart from second-order conditions, the preceding analysis also ignores externalities, that is, benefits or costs that are not accurately reflected by money prices. If there are externalities, a purely competitive general equilibrium will not result in an optimal allocation of resources. Externalities may, however, also occur under monopoly or other forms of market structure, and the analysis in this chapter will be confined to a comparison of pricing behavior under different market structures in the absence of externalities.

Importance of Income Distribution

The relevance of income distribution, and the limitations of rule three, can be explained with the aid of Figure 10–1. TT, which is usually referred to as a production-possibility curve, represents the maximum alternative combinations of two goods, X and Y, which can be produced by a given amount of resources. The problem of securing an optimal allocation of resources between the production of X and Y is to select a point on TT which is the best point in some sense.

The slope at any point on the production-possibility curve equals the marginal rate of transformation (MRT) of X into Y. It indicates how many additional Y can be produced by reducing output of X by one unit and transferring resources to Y production. A point on TT which satisfies the condition that the MRS between X and Y of every

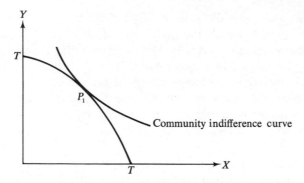

Figure 10–1　Diagrammatic Representation of Optimal Resource Allocation

member of society equals MRT can be depicted diagrammatically as a point at which a community indifference curve is tangent to that point, such as P_1 in Figure 10–1.

A community indifference curve (hereafter abbreviated to CIC) shows combinations of X and Y which yield unchanged amounts of satisfaction to all members of society. In order to understand fully the limitations of rule three, and the assumption which is implicit in any statement that P_1 is an optimal resource allocation, it is necessary to understand the way in which a CIC is related to income distribution.

The total output of X and Y implied by any given point P on TT can be allocated between members of society in many different ways. Assuming, for expositional convenience only, that there are two members of society, A and B, the preferences of the two can be exhibited by two sets of indifference curves, labeled $a_1, a_2 \ldots$ and $b_1, b_2 \ldots$, respectively. An indifference curve depicts different combinations of two goods yielding the same amount of satisfaction to an individual. Higher subscripts associated with any indifference curve denote higher levels of satisfaction for the individual concerned. Allocations of the output P between the two members which satisfy rule one are numerous. The locus of such allocations is called the contract curve. At any particular point on this curve the ratio of the marginal utilities of X and Y is the same for each member of society but this ratio generally differs in value at different points on the contract curve. The total output corresponding to some point P on TT, the preferences of A and B, and the contract curve are depicted diagrammatically in Figure 10–2.

Choosing a point P on the production possibility curve TT, we have dropped perpendiculars to both axes of the diagram, so that the sides of the rectangle represent the total amount of each good produced at point P. In the rectangle $OYPX$ are drawn two sets of indifference curves, those of A, relative to the origin O, and those of B, relative

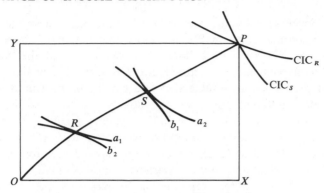

Figure 10-2 Total Output, Individual Preferences, Contract Curve, and Community Indifference Curves

to the origin *P*. The contract curve, *ORSP*, is the locus of points of tangency between the indifference curves of A and B.

A CIC through *P* is derived by selecting a point on the contract curve and sliding B's individual indifference curve at that point up and down A's indifference curve at that point, ensuring that the B curve is at all times tangential to the A curve. The upper right-hand corner of the box diagram, which is fixed in relation to B's indifference curve, will trace out combinations of X and Y yielding the same satisfaction to each member as the combination *P* itself. That is, each point on a CIC curve is obtained by adding a combination of X and Y corresponding to a point on one of A's indifference curves to a combination of X and Y corresponding to a point on one of B's indifference curves, ensuring that the individual indifference curves have the same slope at the chosen points. Different points on the CIC curve correspond to differently sloped points on the two selected individual indifference curves. The slope of the CIC at any point will equal the slope of the mutually tangent individual indifference curves from which that point was derived; at *P*, for example, the slope of the CIC through *P* equals the slope of the mutually tangent individual indifference curves at the chosen point on the contract curve.

There will be a different CIC through *P* corresponding to every different point on the contract curve. Each of these CICs will pass through *P* at a different angle if, as is generally assumed to be the case, the slope of the mutually tangent individual indifference curves is different at different points on the contract curve.

Different points on the contract curve represent divisions of the total output of X and Y implied by point P which involve more of both goods for one member of the community and less of both goods for the other. Therefore, different points on the contract curve represent different levels of individual welfare for the members of society; a move along the contract curve makes one individual better off at the expense of the other. The level of welfare of each member of the community implied by a point on the contract curve is termed a welfare distribution. Since satisfaction is subjective and cannot be measured, one cannot compare different points on the contract curve, that is, different welfare distributions. A's loss (gain) of welfare resulting from a move along the contract curve cannot be compared with B's gain (loss). Therefore, in the absence of any generally agreed rule for the ranking of welfare distributions, no comparisons may be made between the CICs derived from different points on the contract curve, since each is associated with a different welfare distribution.

We return now to consider Figure 10–1. The slope of the CIC through P_1, the rate at which every member of the community would be willing to exchange one good for the other, depends upon the allocation of the total output P_1 between members of the community. Conversely, the fact that a particular CIC is tangent to TT at a particular point (such as P_1) implies a particular division of output P_1 between members of the group, and therefore a level of welfare for each member of the group. The income distribution will, for a community consisting of two members, correspond to that point on the contract curve where the slope of the members' individual indifference curves is equal to the slope of the CIC which is tangent at P_1. The level of individual welfare implicit in such an income distribution will be shown by the mutually tangent individual indifference curves at that point. Given the level of welfare for each member of society implied by this distribution of income, P_1 is the best point on TT —it is impossible by shifting resources to increase the satisfaction of any member of the community without reducing the satisfaction of some other member.

The assertion, however, that a point on TT such as P_1, at which a CIC is tangent, is the best allocation of resources implies a value judgment that the division of the output and resulting welfare distribution implicit in that CIC is the best. Changing the income distribution will change the slope of the CIC through P_1, and hence the optimality of the resource allocation at P_1. For each point on TT representing a combination of goods, there is a unique distribution of those goods between the members of the community which invests that point with the properties of an optimum, that is, which will result in a CIC being tangent to TT at that point. In Figure 10–3, for example, P_1, P_2, and P_3 are points on TT which satisfy rule three. Each of these points represents an optimal allocation of resources between the production of different goods, given the distribution of goods among members of the

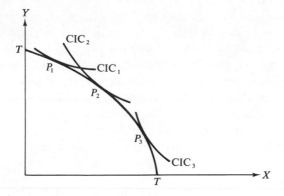

Figure 10–3 Optimal Resource Allocation with Different Welfare Distributions

community and hence the level of individuals' welfare implied by the slope of the CIC at each point. Since the welfare distribution implicit in each CIC is different, that is, some people are better off and others worse off at the different points P_1, P_2, and P_3, the points themselves cannot be compared.

The preceding analysis enables us to point to another limitation of rule three. An allocation of resources which satisfies the requirements of rule three cannot be said to be superior to *any* allocation of resources which violates rule three. Two such allocations are represented, respectively, by points P_1 and P_2 in Figure 10–4.

Of the point P_1, it may be asserted that, with the particular division of the output implied by the slope of CIC_1 at point P_1, it is impossible to increase the satisfaction of some members of the community without reducing that of other members, by shifting resources and producing

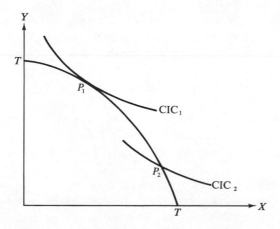

Figure 10–4 Incomparable Resource Allocations

a different combination of outputs. This statement, however, does not hold for point P_2, for by shifting resources from the production of X into the production of Y, hence moving from P_2 to some other point on TT, it would be possible to make some members of the community better off without making others worse off. Unless, however, the CICs through P_1 and P_2 reflect Pareto-comparable welfare distributions, the two resource allocations cannot be compared, and therefore P_1 cannot be said to be superior to P_2. The term "Pareto-comparable" refers to welfare distributions which differ from each other merely in that some people are better off under one distribution than another, but no one is worse off.

Monopoly and Resource Allocation

Much discussion among economists about public policy directed against monopoly is based upon the implicit assumption that monopoly pricing behavior results in an allocation of resources which does not maximize welfare in the Pareto sense. It is appropriate, therefore, to investigate whether monopoly behavior violates the three rules outlined in first section of this chapter.

Rule one will not be violated if monopolists charge the same price for any particular product to all consumers. Because each (maximizing) consumer chooses that combination of goods which equates his MRS between any pair of goods with the ratio of their prices, an economy, whether competitive or monopolistic, which charges the same price for each commodity to every consumer will equate the MRS of different consumers and therefore lead to an efficient allocation of output among consumers.

Rule one will be violated, however, if a monopolist charges a different price for the same commodity to different consumers. Because each maximizing consumer chooses that combination of goods which results in an equality between the ratio of marginal utilities of any two goods and the price ratio of those goods, different price ratios confronting different consumers as a result of monopoly price discrimination will mean that the ratio of marginal utilities of two goods differs for different consumers. That is, it would be possible for consumers to exchange products and thereby increase the total satisfaction they derive from a given total output.

If a monopolist in selling markets is also a monopsonist (single buyer) in input markets, so that the price which the monopolist has to pay for inputs is influenced by the scale of its input purchases, then it is likely that rule two will be violated. A purely competitive firm cannot influence the price it pays for inputs and in order to minimize the cost of producing its selected output level will select a combination of inputs which equates the ratio of the marginal physical productivities of each pair of inputs with the price ratio of the inputs. In contrast, in order to minimize the cost of producing any given level of output, a monopsonist will hire a combination of inputs which equates the ratio of the marginal physical productivities of any pair of inputs with the ratio of *marginal input costs,* not the ratio of input prices. Although, in equilibrium, all firms in the economy pay the same price per unit of any particular input, the ratio of marginal input costs to different firms will differ from the price ratio of the inputs, unless, by chance, the elasticity of supply of any input is the same for all firms. Apart from this last situation, it follows therefore that the ratio of the marginal physical productivities of any two inputs will be different in different firms, so that rule two is violated. The combination of inputs selected by the monopsonist will be inefficient in the sense that rule two is violated and, by using a different combination of inputs and reallocating inputs between firms, the same level of aggregate output could be produced with fewer resources.

It must be stressed that the above argument does not depend in any way upon a failure by the monopsonist to attempt to minimize the money cost of producing any particular level of output. A pure competitor must maximize profits in order to survive; a monopolist may pursue objectives other than profit maximization, such as sales revenue maximization for example. The pursuit of objectives other than profit maximization does not, however, imply absence of an attempt to minimize the cost of producing any given level of output. In the case of the sales revenue maximizer, for example, it was pointed out in Chapter 1 that the need to make some profits acts as a constraint. A reduction in the cost of producing output and consequent increase in profits will enable the firm to satisfy the constraint and yet increase sales revenue. Hence, in order to show why monopolists should not be efficient in the sense of minimizing the total cost of producing any level of output they produce, it is not sufficient to point out that they pursue objectives other than profit maximization; instead it must be shown, for example, that the incentive to minimize costs is reduced.

Finally, we turn to rule three. The two preceding sections demonstrate that a system of pricing which results in output levels involving different price-marginal cost ratios for different products implies that the marginal rate of substitution in consumption is not equal to the marginal rate of transformation in production. Given the distribution of welfare implicit in such a price system and resulting allocation of resources, it would be possible to make some members of the community better off without making anyone worse off, by shifting resources from the production of those goods where the ratio of price to marginal cost is lowest to those goods where the ratio of price to marginal cost is highest.

A monopoly in an otherwise purely competitive economy therefore leads to a misallocation of resources. Likewise, even though no sectors of the economy are purely competitive, differences in price-marginal cost ratios imply a misallocation of resources in the Pareto sense. The reader might well wonder whether an economy composed of monopolies in final product markets, and where the ratio of price to marginal cost is the same in every industry, is just as efficient from the point of view of allocative efficiency as a purely competitive system in which price equals marginal cost in all sectors. Because the price ratio of each pair of goods will equal the ratio of the marginal costs of producing the goods, marginal rates of substitution in consumption will equal marginal rates of transformation in production *provided* the ratio of marginal costs of each pair of goods corresponds to the marginal rate at which one good can be transformed into the other by a reallocation of resources. This provision will be met only if the marginal cost of any particular input is the same to firms producing either of the goods in question. This, in turn, requires either that there is pure competition in factor markets so that input supply curves facing individual firms are horizontal, or that the elasticity of supply of any particular input is the same for all firms. Even if one of these conditions is satisfied, and marginal cost ratios reflect marginal rates of transformation, a world of monopolies with equal price-marginal cost ratios in final product markets is not quite as efficient from the point of view of allocative efficiency as a world of pure competition; there will be a misallocation of resources between the production of leisure and the production of all other goods. This can be explained as follows. Leisure is one of the commodities every individual can consume. Other goods are obtained by trading leisure (hours of work offered) for money incomes with which to buy other goods. In order to maximize satisfaction from consuming commodities and leisure, an individual must obtain as much satisfaction from the income earned as a result of his last (say) hour's effort as he obtains from the last hour of leisure. If this condition is violated, the individual can, by definition, increase his total satisfaction by working less (having more leisure), or the converse. This is the same as saying that the maximizing individual will equate the ratio of marginal utilities of income (other goods) and leisure with the ratio of their prices. Since the price of one unit of leisure is the wage forgone by having leisure, this condition can be expressed algebraically as

$$\frac{MU_{leisure}}{MU_{other\ goods}} = \frac{Wage}{P_{other\ goods}}$$

Firms, on the other hand, in order to maximize profits, will hire a quantity of labor which equates the marginal revenue from employing labor to the marginal cost of labor which, in the absence of monopsony in the labor market, equals the wage paid per unit of labor. Firms in pure competition will therefore hire a quantity of labor which satisfies the following condition:

$$Wage = MPP^{labor}_{other\ goods} \times P_{other\ goods}$$

that is,

$$\frac{Wage}{P_{og}} = MPP^{labor}_{other\ goods}$$

The expression $MPP^{labor}_{other\ goods}$ is the rate of transforming one unit of leisure into other goods—the marginal rate of technical transformation (MRT). Because $MPP^{labor}_{other\ goods}$ equals $Wage/P_{og}$, which in turn equals $MU_{leisure}/MU_{other\ goods}$, it follows that $MRT = MRS$, and rule three dealing with allocative efficiency is satisfied.

In a world of monopolies in final product markets, however, firms will, in order to maximize profits, hire a quantity of labor which satisfies the following condition:

$$Wage = MPP^{labor}_{other\ goods} \times Marginal\ revenue_{other\ goods}$$

that is,

$$\frac{Wage}{MR_{og}} = MPP^{labor}_{other\ goods}$$

Because $MPP^{labor}_{other\ goods}$ equals $Wage/MR_{og}$, which is greater than $Wage/P_{og}$, it follows that, in equilibrium, the rate at which leisure can be transformed into other goods ($=MRT$) exceeds the number of units of other goods for which consumers are willing to give up one unit of leisure ($=MRS$). The allocation of resources between leisure and the production of other goods is nonoptimal since it is possible by shifting resources out of production of leisure into the production of other goods to make some people better off without making others worse off.

It must be stressed that the preceding arguments against monopoly in no way rest upon the argument that monopoly distorts income distribution. This argument, sometimes put forward against monopoly, is operationally meaningless in the absence of a universally acceptable criterion of ideal income distribution. The point of the preceding analysis is that under *any* income distribution, monopoly combined with pure competition, or uneven degrees of monopoly resulting in different price-marginal cost relationships, will result in a misallocation of resources in the Pareto sense. That is, it would be possible, *without altering the existing income distribution*, to make some members of the community better off without making anyone worse off, by reallocating resources and altering the distribution of output among members of the community.

Before we leave the subject of monopoly and resource allocation, it is appropriate to mention briefly the theory of second best, which may be summarized as follows. Comparing two maximization (or minimization) problems that are identical in all respects except that a constraint is introduced into the second problem which prevents the attainment of at least one of the optimal conditions in the solution to the first problem, the optimal values of the variables in the second problem will, in general, differ from those in the unconstrained problem.

The implications of the theory of second best for the problem of monopoly versus pure competition are as follows. The rules of Pareto optimality will only be satisfied if there is pure competition in every sector of an economy, so that marginal cost equals price in every sector. If a constraint prevents the attainment of one or more Paretian conditions, the theory of second best indicates that the remaining Paretian conditions are in general no longer desirable. Thus, for example, if the condition that marginal cost equals price cannot be established for some firms in the economy, the second best optimum requires that this equality be departed from in other firms. In a mixed economy with some industries not operating under conditions of pure competition, it may be undesirable in terms of economic welfare to attempt to restructure some but not all of these monopolistic industries. The theory of second best indicates that there is no a priori way to judge between various situations in which some of the Paretian optimum conditions are fulfilled while others are not, and that it is not true that a situation in which more, but not all, of the optimum conditions are fulfilled is necessarily, or even likely to be, superior to a situation in which fewer are fulfilled. To apply to only part of an economy welfare rules which would lead to a Pareto optimum if they were applied everywhere, may move the economy away from, not toward, a second best optimum position.

Importance of Firms' Objectives

When comparing the Pareto optimality of resource allocation under conditions of pure competition and monopoly, it is assumed that firms in either situation pursue the objective of profit maximization. The question arises, what are the implications of the pursuit of alternative objectives for comparisons of different market situations with regard to their Pareto optimality? It is impossible to give a complete answer to this question without discussing every conceivable objective and its implications for the behavior of an individual firm. It is perhaps appropriate, however, to mention the implications of one or two alternative objectives.

The pursuit of some alternative objectives may lead to similar behavior, in terms of price-cost relationships, to that of a profit maximizer, and will not therefore invalidate the conclusions based on a comparison of purely competitive and monopolistic market situations reached in the preceding sections. As indicated in Chapter 1, if firms pursue growth rate maximization objectives, equilibrium price-cost relationships will be the same as would result from profit-maximizing objectives. That is, the firms will produce a level of output which maximizes profits in any current period; the only difference between the growth rate and profit maximizer will be the rate at which the firm expands its total operations through time.

In other circumstances, however, the pursuit of other objectives may invalidate conclusions based upon the profit-maximization hypothesis. For example, as indicated in Chapter 1, a sales revenue maximizer will produce a larger level of output in any particular period than a profit maximizer unless the profit constraint equals the maximum attainable profits. How does this affect a comparison of the Pareto optimality of purely competitive, and monopolistic markets? Empirical evidence suggests that average costs are constant in the neighborhood of output levels chosen by many firms; in these circumstances marginal cost equals average cost. Provided that the price-average cost ratio of all sales revenue maximizers is the same, it would then follow, since $AC = MC$, that the price-marginal cost ratios of different firms will also be identical—which is what is required in order to obtain an optimal allocation of resources between the production of different goods according to the Pareto criterion.[1] That is, if average costs are

---

[1] Assuming that marginal cost ratios reflect marginal rates of transformation, and ignoring the leisure-other goods aspect of resource allocation.

constant, price-marginal cost ratios will be the same for all firms if the minimum unit profit constraint, indicated by P/AC, is the same for all firms. Such a requirement could conceivably be enforced by the capital market; that is, shareholders might not provide finance for particular firms unless the profit rate obtained on investment in productive activities is similar to that obtainable in other firms. In these circumstances, provided that the profit constraint in monopolistic industries equals that in purely competitive industries, constrained sales-revenue-maximizing behavior by firms in both types of industry may lead to an optimal resource allocation between different goods, excepting the leisure–other goods aspect of resource allocation. That is, there may be no reason for preferring one form of market structure to another, or for preferring a homogeneous economy to a mixed economy consisting of monopolies and purely competitive industries, from the point of view of allocative efficiency.

Public Policy and Pricing Behavior

The philosophy underlying public policy towards industry is not always clear; nonetheless, it is undoubtedly influenced by economic theory. There seems to be a presumption that monopoly pricing behavior results in a misallocation of resources; this presumption is based largely upon orthodox economic theory, as already outlined in the preceding sections.

A group of independent firms may, perhaps by colluding, price or determine output as though the industry they form were a monopoly. There is, in general, a presumption that agreements between independent firms with respect to prices, terms, quantities, or markets served, are against the public interest. In the United States, for example, price agreements are illegal per se. In Great Britain, a slightly different approach is taken; price agreements have to be registered and are presumed to be against the public interest unless the parties to the agreement can demonstrate, to the satisfaction of the Restrictive Practices Court, that the agreement is in the public interest.

Instead of agreeing explicitly on prices or other terms, independent firms may be parties to open price or price information agreements. In these circumstances the firms agree to notify each other of prices and conditions of sale and changes therein, and often agree to supply other relevant information such as costs and turnover. An important question facing public policy makers is how these agreements are likely to affect the behavior of the firms who are parties to the agreement.

A number of economists have attempted to show that such agreements can improve competition. It has been argued, for example, that the exchange of price information avoids "phantom competition," the quoting by customers of other firms' prices at lower levels than the true ones in order to persuade the seller to reduce his price; in reply, other economists have argued that far less information than is usually provided under information agreements is needed to overcome this problem. Some writers have claimed that information agreements reduce uncertainty and permit more orderly investment planning; in reply, others have pointed out that although reduced uncertainty may permit more efficient but less flexible machinery to be installed, for example, it may also, by reducing the profitability of a price cut, deter investment in more efficient methods of production. Finally, some economists have suggested that information agreements will help to avoid the misdirection of competitive efforts; it can also be argued, however, that uncertainty about rivals' reactions may foster concern by entrepreneurs with more efficient methods. The threat of price competition may strengthen the incentive to innovate, for example.

The most important effect of the exchange of price or other information by sellers is that, by providing firms with information about which they would otherwise have been in doubt, the expected reaction of a firm's rivals is made more certain. In Chapter 4 it was pointed out that the pricing behavior of a firm will be influenced by the firm's expectations regarding the reactions of its rivals to its own policies. At one extreme, if a firm believes that its rivals are unaware of its prices, then it will be less likely to consider their reactions to its pricing decision than if it knows that they are fully informed. Under a price-information agreement, secret changes are by definition ruled out, hence the expected reaction must be considered.

Although there is much controversy about the economic consequences of price-information agreements, most observers agree that collusion becomes easier where price or other information is exchanged; however, whether it is more likely to occur remains controversial. The United States has a tradition of per se condemnation of explicit price agreements, but the circulation of prices is not condemned per se. The American approach is one of attempting to discover whether collusion actually exists with respect to the price charged. The courts have been reluctant to infer collusion from mere uniformity of prices charged; other factors suggesting collusion must usually be present, such as express agreement not to deviate from published prices, or meetings to discuss price and output policies.

It must be stressed, however, that price-information agreements may affect pricing behavior even though there is no collusion whatever between the parties to the information agreement. The mere fact of dissemination may affect pricing behavior; all that is required is that the information agreement change a firm's expectations regarding rivals' reactions. As explained in Chapters 4 and 7, monopoly pricing by firms in a particular industry can occur without collusion of any kind. By entering into a price-information agreement, firms voluntarily give up the advantage of surprise attack in return for similar assurances from their rivals. In these circumstances, retaliation can be immediate, and a firm will only cut price when it believes that other firms will not do so, or that even though they do, it will not help them.

The relation of prices to costs is one important aspect of industry behavior; the rapidity of the response of prices to changes in supply and demand conditions is a related matter. Changes in tastes, or technology, will mean that the optimal allocation of resources changes through time. Price agreements, or price-information agreements, may reduce the flexibility of prices in response to such changes, and therefore hinder the achievement of an optimal resource allocation.

Before leaving the subject of public policy and pricing behavior, we shall analyze price-discrimination practices in order to illustrate the complications involved in attempting to apply economic analysis to particular problems of public policy: If different consumers pay different prices for the same good, the ratio of marginal utilities of that good and other goods will differ for different consumers and rule one, the rule of distributive efficiency, will be violated. Can it be concluded that abolition of price discrimination would be an unambiguous improvement in the situation? The answer is no. Let us assume, for the moment, that abolition of price discrimination will not change the level of output. Although it is true that it would be *possible* to improve the welfare of some members of the community without making others worse off, it cannot be assumed that this would occur merely as a result of making price discrimination illegal. The resulting price changes will probably change income distribution, and therefore welfare distribution. If the total market is originally divided into two submarkets, abolition of price discrimination will increase price in the market where demand is more elastic. In the absence of any other changes, the real income, and therefore welfare, of buyers in that market will be reduced. Additional policies, such as redistributions of money income are necessary in order to ensure that no one suffers a reduction in welfare. Second, it is possible that abolition of price discrimination will change the level of output of the product. In these circumstances, price discrimination can only be judged by comparing the output mix with and without price discrimination. The problem cannot be solved by invoking rule one only. Suppose, for example, that output is greater with price discrimination than without price discrimination, and that in the absence of price discrimination the ratio of price to marginal cost is higher in this industry than elsewhere in the economy. Given the existing welfare distribution, this might imply that the allocation of resources could be improved by increasing the output of the product—that is, discriminating monopoly may move resource allocation closer to optimal than absence of price discrimination, despite the fact that it would be possible to allocate the output mix resulting under discrimination more efficiently between members of the community.

Public Policy and Mergers

A number of countries have adopted public policy measures which restrict merger between formerly independent firms in certain circumstances. In the United States, for example, Section 7 of the Clayton Act, as amended by the 1950 Celler-Kefauver Antimerger Act, forbids mergers which tend to lessen competition substantially, or tend to create a monopoly, in any line of commerce. The Clayton Act applies not only to so-called horizontal mergers between firms operating at the same stage in the production and distribution of a particular product, but also to vertical mergers between firms at successive stages in the production of a particular product, and to conglomerate mergers between firms producing different products.

We shall not be concerned with how the courts have interpreted and applied the law affecting mergers, but instead consider briefly the underlying economic rationale of merger policy, distinguishing between horizontal, vertical, and conglomerate mergers.

In order to judge whether a particular merger is likely to lessen competition substantially in practice, the relevant market must be defined, because whether behavior will be influenced depends upon the number and size distribution of firms operating in the relevant market. As indicated in Chapter 2, if one is interested in the behavior of firms, the relevant market should be defined to include products of firms whose behavior is likely to affect each other significantly and whose behavior will therefore be interrelated.

Apart from the problem of defining the relevant market, answering the question of whether merger will lessen competition is not without its problems. Horizontal merger between two firms operating in the same market reduces the number of firms in that market, and this may influence industry behavior. Confining ourselves for the moment to pricing behavior, a priori theory does not, however, indicate that industry behavior will necessarily be worsened by a reduction in the number of firms in an industry. Smaller numbers may make firms more aware of interdependence and therefore lead to more monopolistic pricing behavior; on the other hand it may not do so. The number of firms in the market will of course be an important determinant of whether this is likely to be the case. With very small numbers, interdependence may already have been recognized and taken into account prior to merger, and merger may therefore have no effect upon industry behavior. With very large numbers, behavior may also be unaffected if the number of firms remaining after merger is still large enough to lead firms to ignore each other in their individual policymaking. Apart from the effect on numbers, the effect of merger on the size distribution of firms in an industry may be a more important determinant of industry behavior in certain circumstances, and a reduction in numbers may be accompanied by a change in size distribution which improves industry pricing performance despite increased awareness of interdependence. Merger between two small firms, for example, may enable them to compete more effectively with larger firms dominating the relevant market.

The effect of vertical mergers upon pricing behavior at each stage of the productive process has been discussed at length in Chapter 8, and will not be repeated here. It is sufficient to remind the reader that vertical integration may either increase or reduce the price of the final product and that it is impossible to generalize about the effect of vertical integration by merger on industry pricing performance.

Finally, we turn to the question of how conglomerate mergers between firms producing different products are likely to influence behavior in individual product markets. Whether industry behavior will be changed by such mergers depends upon whether the merged firms will act in a different manner from the manner in which they acted individually prior to merger, or whether other firms in individual product markets expect them to act differently. The belief is widely held that a diversified firm, by virtue of its multiplicity of geographic and product markets, has a competitive advantage over a firm producing and selling in only one of those markets. This belief seems to be founded upon the notion that a diversified firm can subsidize the cost of products sold in some markets out of the profits earned in other markets, thereby placing the firms operating only in the subsidized markets at a competitive disadvantage and either driving them out of business or reducing their profits and growth rate. Unless capital requirement or other entry barriers exist to prevent a single-product firm from diversifying into the subsidizing markets, however, it is difficult to see how any competitive advantage can exist for diversified firms.

The preceding discussion has been confined to analyzing the influence of merger on industry pricing performance. Even if the pricing performance is worsened by merger, smaller numbers may mean an increase in other forms of competition, and an improvement in other dimensions of industry performance, such as R&D or other aspects of product policy. Unfortunately, for reasons explained in the following sections, we lack criteria for judging these other aspects of industry performance; for the present, therefore, public policy must necessarily confine itself to evaluating the effect of merger on pricing performance only.

A number of arguments are sometimes put forward in defense of mergers. One defense of merger is limited to those cases in which bankruptcy or liquidation seem imminent. The so-called failing company defense, recognized by the United States courts, is based upon the idea that if a firm is failing, it is no longer a vital competitive factor in the market. There are obvious problems involved in trying to apply such a doctrine. What is the appropriate criterion, for example, for judging whether a company has failed enough to justify a merger? A firm may even be failing precisely because of the predatory tactics of another firm wishing to take it over.

Another prominent defense of merger is the argument that merger may increase efficiency and reduce the cost of producing an industry's output either by permitting scale economies to be reaped or by eliminating other inefficiencies. Profits depend upon costs in addition to revenues, and even though merger may not affect the level of industry price and revenue, it may increase efficiency and industry profits. If merger were the only way to achieve economies in cost, the merger might also change industry pricing behavior and worsen allocative efficiency even though it improved technical efficiency, and the public-policy maker would be confronted with the problem of choosing between these two aspects of economic efficiency. Some economists have argued that such a conflict need not arise because if increased efficiency is really the motive for merger it can be achieved through internal expansion of a single firm, and that any important economies attained through merger can always be gained through internal growth. It must be pointed out, however, that in order to improve through internal expansion of an individual firm the efficiency with which a given level of industry output is produced, other firms must contract and/or be eliminated from the industry. Price competition by the expanding firm is a means of accomplishing this. In some circumstances, however, there may be no incentive to eliminate inefficiencies through internal expansion. In the case of an oligopolistic industry composed of a few strong firms and characterized by absence of price competition, for example, merger may be the only means of eliminating inefficiencies, since expansion and price competition initiated by one firm is unlikely to occur.

A more recent defense[2] of mergers consists of the argument that

---

[2] See H. G. Manne, reference (7).

mergers are a device safeguarding shareholders' interests by forcing managers to be efficient and maximize profits. The market price of a firm's shares will, it is argued, be correlated with the profits earned by the firm. If a firm is poorly managed, in the sense of not making as great a return for the shareholders as could be accomplished under other feasible managements, the market price of the shares will be low relative to the market price of shares of other firms in the same industry or relative to the market as a whole. The lower the share price, relative to what it could be with other more efficient management, the more attractive a take-over becomes to those who believe that they can manage the firm more efficiently. The threat of take-over will, it is argued, act as a spur to management efficiency.

Furthermore, it can be argued that the managers of *competing* firms are likely to have more information crucial to take-over decisions, such as cost conditions in their own firms. Reliable information is also available to a firm's suppliers and customers. For these reasons, many horizontal and vertical mergers may be of this control take-over variety rather than the foreclosure of competitors or scale economies type.

While this argument is a plausible hypothesis, the problem confronting the public policy maker is that of devising methods for distinguishing mergers motivated by a quest for monopoly profits from those merely trying to establish efficient management in poorly run companies. Industry profits depend not only upon costs, but also upon revenues. Higher profits may be anticipated, not because of increased efficiency and lower costs in the firm taken over, but because of higher anticipated revenues resulting from more monopolistic industry pricing after merger than existed in the industry prior to merger. Alternatively, anticipated profits may be increased for both reasons, in which case the dilemma of choosing between greater technical efficiency at the expense of less allocative efficiency confronts the public policy maker once again.

Public Policy and Advertising Activities

In Chapter 5, advertising was introduced into the analysis of a firm's behavior as an input that affects the demand for the firm's product. While public policy towards pricing behavior is based, at least in part, upon conclusions derived from economic theory, the same cannot be said of policy towards advertising. Economic theory provides no clear public policy guide lines in the case of advertising. Few people would deny that a clear case can be made for laws to protect consumers against false or misleading advertising; what, however, can be said regarding levels of advertising which do not fall into this category?

Advertising is frequently treated with hostility by laymen and economists alike. The argument that advertising outlays are too high in particular industries, such as the pharmaceutical industry, is frequently heard. Distrust of advertising stems from comparative neglect, fostered by economic theory itself, of the benefits of advertising from the point of view of buyers of advertised products, as opposed to the benefits to sellers of these products. Traditional economic theory assumes that knowledge is perfect—that consumers are fully aware of the nature of all products offered by producers, and the prices of the products. This assumption is not a valid description of the real world. Information regarding available products is not a free good, automatically available to anyone and everyone. In the absence of advertising, buyers must acquire information in other ways, ways which might conceivably be more costly, from the buyer's point of view, than the cost of resources devoted to advertising, which must be recouped in the prices of advertised products. Referring back to the rules of optimal resource and product allocation in the first section of this chapter, advertising may be a means of achieving these optimal conditions by providing buyers with information regarding available products and their terms of sale, at lower cost than alternative methods of obtaining information.

A distinction is sometimes made between informative and persuasive advertising, the implication being that the former is desirable while the latter is undesirable. Unfortunately, this provides no additional guide lines for public policy, for it is impossible to give any operationally significant meaning to the two terms. Conceptually, the difference between the two types of advertising is that informative advertising enables buyers to satisfy existing preferences by informing them of available alternatives, while persuasive advertising changes preferences. In practice, however, preferences are necessarily formed on the basis of information; whether such information is informative or persuasive is a matter of semantics. Nor is it possible to evaluate the level of advertising associated with particular products with reference to whether the price of the product is reduced or increased. In Chapter 5 it was explained that advertising might either increase price, or, by permitting firms to reap economies of scale in production, might reduce the price of a product. Even though price is increased, however, the cost of the product plus the cost of obtaining information regarding the nature of the product, may be lower to buyers than in the absence of advertising.

Advertising itself uses resources; viewed in this context the problem of evaluating levels of advertising becomes a special case in the problem of resource allocation. The relevant question then, is whether the benefits of advertising, from the point of view of the members of the community, at least equal the benefits that could be obtained if the resources used in advertising were used for other purposes. An answer to this question requires that the benefits of advertising be measured and compared with the benefits resulting from alternative uses of resources devoted to advertising. Unfortunately, the problem of defining and measuring the benefits of advertising has not yet been solved. As a result, the problem of determining how many resources to devote to advertising is a question which, in its current state, economic theory cannot answer. Some questions relating to advertising may not, however, require the measurement of actual benefits associated with the information provided. For example, it may be possible to determine whether the same information provided by current levels of advertising could be provided more efficiently, in terms of resources used, by other methods, while leaving the question of how many resources to devote to providing information until such time as the analytical tools required to provide an answer to this question have been forged.

Although economic theory provides no clear guide lines for public policy towards advertising itself, what can be said of the relationship between advertising and other aspects of firms' behavior, such as pricing and price-cost relationships? Some empirical evidence[3] reveals that the prices of advertised goods tend to be higher than those of unadvertised goods. However, as already explained, the cost of the advertised product, including information, may be lower for buyers of these products than in the absence of advertising. If this were not so, there would seem little reason why advertised products should survive in competition with unadvertised brands. A more important consideration than the height of price is the relationship between advertising and price-cost margins. Does advertising, for example, foster monopoly by creating barriers to entry which permit monopoly pricing? Advertising may increase barriers to entry into an industry if, in order to enter the industry, potential entrants must spend more on advertising per unit of output than established firms spend, because this implies an absolute cost disadvantage of potential entrants compared to established firms. Alternatively, advertising can increase entry barriers if advertising is characterized by economies of scale, or if the funds to finance advertising can only be obtained at a higher interest rate than that paid by established firms.

Empirical evidence relating to these matters is still scarce, and by no means conclusive. The evidence obtained in one study of advertising[4] indicates that levels of industry advertising and seller concentration are not systematically related. It also suggests that there is negative cor-

---

[3] See, for example, reference (13).
[4] See reference (13).

relation between changes in advertising and industrial concentration; this is consistent with a situation in which new firms break into an industry by advertising, and some economists have stressed that advertising expenditures may be a means by which new competitors can establish themselves rather than a barrier to entry. None of this evidence, however, is inconsistent with the hypothesis that advertising is a barrier to entry and permits monopoly pricing by established firms in an industry. The influence of concentration on price-cost relationships is analytically distinct from that of entry barriers. On the one hand, a priori theory indicates that, other things being equal, higher concentration may be expected to lead to higher industry profit rates; on the other hand, as the analysis in Chapter 7 indicates, price cannot exceed average cost in the long run by more than the height of entry barriers. The relevant question at issue is whether advertising and profit rates are related, not whether advertising and concentration are related.

The evidence presented in a recent statistical study[5] indicates that profit rates and advertising are positively associated. If this positive relationship is a long-run characteristic, this evidence is consistent with the hypothesis that advertising creates entry barriers and permits monopoly pricing. It must be added that the height of entry barriers depends also on other factors in addition to advertising, such as the extent of production economies of scale relative to the size of the market, the absolute amount of capital required to operate a plant of minimum efficient scale, and other absolute production cost disadvantages of new entrants compared to established firms.

The conclusion that advertising may act as a barrier to entry and permit more monopolistic pricing in particular industries is not altered by the finding of some studies that brand shares within industries are less stable, the higher the level of industry advertising, implying that advertising is a means of competition. That is, competition between firms in an industry through advertising is still compatible with poor industry pricing performance as indicated by price-cost relationships.

If advertising is a substitute for price competition, the problem confronting the policy maker is that of choosing between better pricing performance, and lower advertising. In the current state of our knowledge, there are no grounds for preferring good pricing performance to more advertising. That is, there is no reason, in a world of imperfect knowledge and changes in tastes and technology, to believe that price competition is more desirable than advertising. In certain circumstances, advertising may amount to price competition; if, for example, some buyers are purchasing a product at a price higher than the price charged

---

[5] Reference (3).

by another firm about which they are uninformed, advertising which provides this information may reduce the price of the product to these buyers. Even if products were not changing in character with the passage of time, the population of buyers is changing over time, and advertising may be the most efficient means of informing them of alternatives available. Similarly, even if the composition of the buying population were not changing, information regarding changes in the nature of seller's products resulting from technical progress must be transmitted to buyers, and might be transmitted to them most efficiently by advertising messages. Unfortunately, as already mentioned, we are lacking an operational criterion of good advertising performance; in the absence of such a criterion, it is impossible to choose objectively between good pricing behavior and more advertising.

Public Policy and Research and Development Activities

The preceding sections indicate that there is a general presumption in favor of low concentration as a structural goal on the grounds that this is more likely to result in price-cost relationships compatible with efficient resource allocation.

There is disagreement among economists on the question of which form of market structure is most conducive to research activity and technological progress. Some argue that firms with monopoly power are more likely to undertake technological research than firms in highly competitive industries; this argument is based upon the notion that the prospective returns to R&D activities will be higher in the case of firms in the former category, and/or that such firms will have higher profits and hence a larger supply of funds for financing R&D activities. Supporters of the contrary view argue that the competitive influences of atomistic industries will spur the quest for technological advances whereas monopolies, even if they possess greater investment funds, need not employ them in the quest for new technology, and are less likely to do so since competitive pressures are less. Other economists have argued that oligopoly is the market structure most likely to encourage innovation, for such a structure, it is argued, combines the funds to finance R&D with competitive pressures that will cause firms to use the funds to innovate.

What does empirical evidence concerning market structure and R&D activities indicate? A considerable amount of empirical evidence has been gathered concerning the relationship between firm size and innovational input and output. It is undoubtedly true that most R&D is performed by the larger firms in an economy. In part this may be accounted for by the indivisibilities of expensive R&D inputs, already discussed in Chapter 5 in the section entitled Research and Development Activities. However, looking at those firms which carry out R&D, the evidence suggests that beyond a certain size level, the ratio of R&D expenditures to some index of firm size does not increase significantly with firm size, and may even decline. Up to that size level, which varies from industry to industry, innovational effort appears to increase more than proportionately with size. Uncertainty concerning the precise relationship between R&D and firm size among the largest firms in a particular industry is largely attributable to the small number of firms in this category in most industries. The results of any particular statistical study will be greatly influenced by the treatment accorded to each individual observation; different statistical approaches, such as differences in how firms not engaging in R&D activities are dealt with, are capable of yielding different results in terms of the relationship between large firm size and R&D activities.

Large absolute size is not, of course, the same thing as large market power, which depends instead upon absolute size in relation to market size. The available statistical evidence concerning the relationship between market power, measured by concentration, and R&D activities is still rather inconclusive. Industrial research, whether measured by R&D expenditures, employment of scientific and technical personnel, or patented inventions, is heavily concentrated in industries which have moderate to high levels of concentration. However, the industries of relatively high concentration are also the industries in which technological opportunity is greater. That is, the advance of science opens up more possibilities in these industries, and greater technological opportunity, rather than higher concentration, might conceivably account for the greater apparent progressiveness of these industries. The important question is whether, in industries with similar technological opportunity, R&D activities are greater in the more concentrated industries. A recent statistical study[6] suggests that even after interindustry technological opportunity differences are taken into account, there remains a tendency for R&D input, measured by scientific and technical personnel, to increase with concentration at low levels of concentration. This tendency appears to be absent, however, at high levels of concentration; the same study found that when the four-firm concentration ratio exceeds 50 or 55 percent, additional concentration is not associated with increases in R&D input, and may even be associated with a decline in this variable. The main public policy implication of these findings is that policies designed to reduce very high levels of concentration on grounds of pro-

[6] Reference (12).

moting pricing behavior compatible with efficient resource allocation are unlikely to reduce the level of inventive and innovative activity in the economy. R&D inputs will be reduced only if desirable pricing behavior requires a level of concentration lower than the level at which R&D inputs cease to increase with increases in concentration.

Even if the evidence suggested that reduced concentration would reduce R&D activities, this would not necessarily imply that public policies which are designed to reduce concentration should be abandoned, and that the dilemma confronting the public policy maker should always be resolved in favour of more R&D. It cannot be argued that more R&D is in all circumstances better than less R&D. R&D activities require resources which could be used for alternative purposes, and it is impossible to speak meaningfully of technological progress being too slow or too fast without first making quite explicit the general principle by which the distribution of resources between innovational uses and other uses is to be decided. Since the problem is precisely analogous to that of securing an optimal allocation of resources—merely a special case of this problem—it is not immediately obvious that principles similar to those employed in orthodox economic theory and discussed in the first section of this chapter should be rejected. We reject entirely the view of some economists who have argued that aspects of economic performance such as economic progress have nothing to do with the efficiency of use of scarce resources.

These issues are, however, still extremely controversial and a number of problems remain to be solved. In order to devise public policy with respect to R&D activities, it is necessary to show what principles must be applied to determine the right amount of R&D and resulting rate of technological progress in a particular industry, and what kinds of market structure will lead to these optimal levels of R&D. Until these problems have been solved, the goal of adequate progressiveness will continue to lack operational meaning for purposes of policy making.

In view of the preceding comments, it is appropriate to mention briefly the rationale of the patent system which, whatever its actual effects, is intended to encourage R&D investment and the disclosure of new knowledge by giving to firms exclusive rights to commercial exploitation of inventions and innovations resulting from their R&D efforts. This policy, it must be explained, is not based upon the assumption that more R&D is always better than less. It is based to a large extent upon the assumption that there are externalities associated with the production and dissemination of new knowledge and that this will result in a lower level of R&D and dissemination activities than the community desires, whatever the market structure a firm happens to operate in, unless patent protection is granted. Reference has already been made in the section of this chapter entitled Pure Competition and Resource Allocation to the concept of externalities, defined as benefits or costs not reflected by prices or money costs. The argument in support of patent protection, in brief, is as follows.

The total potential benefits of a given amount of new knowledge, in the form of resource savings and new and improved products, may be spread over a wide area of the economy. These benefits can be realized only if potential users are aware of the new knowledge. In the absence of legal property rights over new knowledge, however, a firm has no incentive to disseminate new knowledge once it exists, and may have little incentive to produce new knowledge by investing in R&D activities.

The level of R&D investment financed and undertaken by a firm will depend upon the money value of the benefits of new knowledge that the firm expects to be able to recoup for itself. In the absence of legal property rights over new knowledge, the magnitude of such recoupable benefits is determined largely by the firm's ability to keep new knowledge secret. Some limit on the unrestricted ability of other firms to use the new knowledge is necessary in order to enable the firm to recoup part of the benefits of new knowledge for itself. If products or processes embodying new knowledge can be imitated immediately by other firms, product prices might be driven down to current production costs, preventing the firm from reaping any of the benefits of the new knowledge and from recouping the R&D outlay which produced the new knowledge.

Even if the ability to keep new knowledge secret for a time results in a situation in which the expected return on R&D investment is sufficient to induce a firm to invest in R&D activities, the potential benefits of the resulting knowledge may be far in excess of the realized benefits. In addition to benefits from the application of new knowledge in the firm's own immediate market area, new knowledge may have applications in a much wider and unanticipated area. These benefits cannot be realized unless potential users are aware of the new knowledge, but the firm has no incentive to disseminate the new knowledge resulting from its R&D activities; as already indicated, secrecy is essential in order to enable the firm to reap benefits in the absence of legal property rights over the new knowledge.

These considerations suggest that, in the absence of property rights over new knowledge, the level of R&D investment will be below the level for which consumers would be willing to pay; patent protection, it is argued, will encourage R&D investment and the disclosure of new knowledge in circumstances in which it would otherwise be kept secret, and will move the output of new knowledge closer to the level that consumers desire.

Concluding Comments

This section summarizes briefly some of the problems that remain to be solved in developing a logically consistent body of public policy measures designed to influence industrial structure.

Existing public policy relies heavily upon economic theory concerning the determinants of pricing behavior. There is, however, much scope for broadening our understanding of the determinants of firms' pricing behavior. Economic theory in its present state is still highly inadequate for purposes of generalizing on such traditional variables as price and level of output in situations involving oligopoly, vertical integration, and conglomerate mergers. The nature of other variables, in addition to cost conditions and concentration, which influence firms' pricing behavior, is another area requiring further study.

The current state of economic theory concerning the determinants of other aspects of firms' behavior, including advertising, product policies, and R&D, is far less satisfactory than current theory concerning the determinants of pricing behavior. There are numerous deficiencies in the theoretical and empirical knowledge concerning the determinants of, and relationship between, the various aspects of nonprice competition. However, much work is currently being undertaken in this field, particularly in the area of R&D activities. Although the individual studies usually treat aspects of firms' behavior in isolation, it is to be hoped that from this work will stem a more general theory of firms' behavior encompassing the relationship between different aspects of a firm's behavior. Development of such a theory is essential in order to permit one to predict the effect of particular public policy measures on different dimensions of a firm's behavior. There is, for example, the problem of possible undesirable side effects on progressiveness, selling costs, and other product policies, of measures designed to eliminate monopolistic pricing performance. The interdependence of various aspects of a firm's behavior makes predictions based upon a neglect of this interdependence extremely hazardous.

The implications of alternative objectives, in addition to profit-maximization, for the behavior of firms is also a potential area for further study and refinement of existing knowledge. As indicated in Chapter 1, although profit maximization may provide an adequate description of behavior for purposes of predicting the sign of changes in variables in response to public policy measures, it may not be adequate when interested in the levels and characteristics of firms' activities corresponding to certain public policy parameters in the economic system.

Even if the determinants of all aspects of firms' behavior were known precisely, the application of public policy requires standards against which existing behavior, or changes in behavior, can be compared. Unfortunately, apart from pricing, we lack standards for judging aspects of firms' behavior, particularly standards for evaluating advertising and product policy performance including R&D activities. While the ideal type of pricing performance, from the point of view of maximizing the aggregate welfare of individuals in the community, has been more or less clearly defined and is backed by a respectable body of analysis, the other types of ideal performance have not yet been defined. In the current state of knowledge, there is no way of ascertaining whether the R&D activities of firms in a particular industry constitutes good or bad performance in a given situation. Similarly a definitive and empirically applicable distinction between desirable and excessive or deficient selling costs is not yet available. Both goals therefore have little current operational meaning for purposes of public policy, and much work remains to be done in these areas.

RECOMMENDED READINGS

1. Bator, F. M., "The Simple Analytics of Welfare Maximization," *American Economic Review,* March 1957. Reprinted in W. Breit and H. M. Hochman (eds.) *Readings in Microeconomics* (New York: Holt, Rinehart and Winston, Inc., 1968).
2. Bishop, R. L., "Monopolistic Competition and Welfare Economics," in R. E. Kuenne (ed.) *Monopolistic Competition Theory: Studies in Impact* (New York: John Wiley & Sons, Inc., 1967).
3. Comanor, W. S., and T. A. Wilson, "Advertising, Market Structure and Performance," *Review of Economics and Statistics,* November 1967.
4. Heflebower, R. B., and G. W. Stocking (eds.) *Readings in Industrial Organization and Public Policy* (Homewood, Ill.: Richard D. Irwin, Inc., 1958). Published under the sponsorship of the American Economic Association.
5. Levin, H. J., (ed.) *Business Organization and Public Policy: A Book of Readings* (New York: Holt, Rinehart and Winston, Inc., 1963).
6. Lipsey, R. G., and K. Lancaster, "The General Theory of Second Best," *Review of Economic Studies,* 1956–57.
7. Manne, H. G., "Mergers and the Market for Corporate Control," *Journal of Political Economy,* April 1965.
8. Markham, J. W., "Market Structure, Business Conduct, and Innovation," *American Economic Review,* Papers and Proceedings, May 1965.
9. Mishan, E. J., "The Principle of Compensation Reconsidered," *Journal of Political Economy,* August 1952, pages 314–317 only.
10. O'Brien, D. P., and D. Swann, "Information Agreements—A Problem in Search of a Policy," *Manchester School of Economics and Social Studies,* September 1966.

11. Scherer, F. M., "Firm Size, Market Structure, Opportunity, and the Output of Patented Inventions," *American Economic Review,* December 1965.

12. ———, "Market Structure and the Employment of Scientists and Engineers," *American Economic Review,* June 1967.

13. Telser, L., "Advertising and Competition," *Journal of Political Economy,* December 1964.

14. Williamson, O. E., "Innovation and Market Structure," *Journal of Political Economy,* February 1965.

INDEX